The Imprisonment
of Obatala

and other plays

OBOTUNDE IJIMERE

The Imprisonment of Obatala

Everyman · Woyengi

AFRICAN WRITERS SERIES
Editorial Adviser · Chinua Achebe

18
The Imprisonment of Obatala and other plays

AFRICAN WRITERS SERIES

1 Chinua Achebe: *Things Fall Apart*
2 Cyprian Ekwensi: *Burning Grass*
3 Chinua Achebe: *No Longer at Ease*
4 Kenneth Kaunda: *Zambia Shall be Free*
5 Cyprian Ekwensi: *People of the City*
6 Peter Abrahams: *Mine Boy*
7 James Ngugi: *Weep Not Child*
8 John Reed and Clive Wake (Editors): *A Book of African Verse*
9 Richard Rive (Editor): *Modern African Prose*
10 Paul Edwards (Editor): *Equiano's Travels*
11 T. M. Aluko: *One Man, One Matchet*
12 William Conton: *The African*
13 Mongo Beti: *Mission to Kala*
14 Richard Rive, Alex La Guma, James Matthews and Alf Wannenburgh: *Quartet*
15 David Cook (Editor): *Origin East Africa*
16 Chinua Achebe: *Arrow of God*
17 James Ngugi: *The River Between*
18 Obotunde Ijimere: *The Imprisonment of Obatala and other plays*
19 Cyprian Ekwensi: *Lokotown and other stories*
20 Mugo Gatheru: *Child of Two Worlds*
21 John Munonye: *The Only Son*
22 Lenrie Peters: *The Second Round*
23 Ulli Beier (Editor): *The Origin of Life and Death*
24 Aubrey Kachingwe: *No Easy Task*
25 Elechi Amadi: *The Concubine*
26 Flora Nwapa: *Efuru*
27 Francis Selormey: *The Narrow Path*
28 David Cook and Miles Lee (Editors): *Short East African Plays*
29 Ferdinand Oyono: *Houseboy*
30 T. M. Aluko: *One Man, One Wife*
31 Chinua Achebe: *A Man of the People*
32 T. M. Aluko: *Kinsman and Foreman*
33 Stanlake Samkange: *On Trial for my Country*
34 Cosmo Pieterse (Editor): *Ten One-Act Plays*
35 Alex La Guma: *A Walk in the Night and other stories*
36 James Ngugi: *A Grain of Wheat*
37 Lenrie Peters: *Satellites*
38 Oginga Odinga: *Not yet Uhuru*
39 Ferdinand Oyono: *The Old Man and the Medal*
40 S. A. Konadu: *A Woman in Her Prime*
41 Amu Djoleto: *The Strange Man*
42 Kofi Awoonor and G. Adali-Mortty (Editors): *Messages — Poems from Ghana*
43 Ayi Kwei Armah: *The Beautyful Ones Are Not Yet Born*
44 Elechi Amadi: *The Great Ponds*
45 John Munonye: *Obi*
46 Dennis Brutus: *Letters to Martha and other poems*
47 Tayeb Salih: *The Wedding of Zein*
48 Bakare Gbadamosi and Ulli Beier: *Not Even God is Ripe Enough*
49 Kwame Nkrumah: *Neo-Colonialism*
50 J. P. Clark: *America, their America*
51 James Ngugi: *The Black Hermit*
52 Sahle Sellassie: *The Afersata*
53 Peter K. Palangyo: *Dying in the Sun*
54 Robert Serumaga: *Return to the Shadows*
55 S. A. Konadu: *Ordained by the Oracle*
56 Flora Nwapa: *Idu*
57 Mbella Sonne Dipoko: *Because of Women*
58 Ulli Beier (Editor): *Political Spider and other stories*
59 Bediako Asare: *Rebel*
60 Luis Bernardo Honwana: *We killed Mangy Dog and other stories*
61 Rems Nna Umeasiegbu: *The Way We Lived*
62 Christopher Okigbo: *Labyrinths*
63 Sembene Ousmane: *God's Bits of Wood*
64 Cosmo Pieterse (Editor): *Seven South African Poets*
65 Duro Ladipo: *Three Plays*
66 Tayeb Salih: *Season of Migration to the North*
67 Nkem Nwankwo: *Danda*
68 Gabriel Okara: *The Voice*
69 Taban lo Liyong: *Fixions*
70 T. M. Aluko: *Chief The Honourable Minister*
71 L. S. Senghor: *Nocturnes*
72 Tchicaya U Tam'si: *Poems*
73 Len Ortzen: *North African Writing*
74 Taban lo Liyong: *Eating Chiefs*
75 Jan Knappert: *Myths and Legends of the Swahili*
76 Wole Soyinka: *The Interpreters*
77 Mongo Beti: *King Lazarus*
78 Cosmo Pieterse (Editor): *Eleven Short African Plays*
79 Driss Chraibi: *Heirs to the Past*
80 Nuruddin Farah: *From a Crooked Rib*
81 Tom Mboya: *The Challenge of Nationhood*
82 Mbella Sonne Dipoko: *A Few Nights and Days*

The Imprisonment of Obatala
and other plays

———◆———

Obotunde Ijimere

English Adaptation by
Ulli Beier

HEINEMANN EDUCATIONAL BOOKS LTD
LONDON · IBADAN · NAIROBI

Heinemann Educational Books Ltd
48 Charles Street, London W1X 8AH
PMB 5205, Ibadan · POB 25080, Nairobi

EDINBURGH MELBOURNE TORONTO
HONG KONG SINGAPORE AUCKLAND

ISBN 0 435 90018 8

This translation © Ulli Beier 1966
First published 1966
Reprinted 1968, 1969, 1970

Printed in Malta by
St Paul's Press Ltd

CONTENTS

Introduction   *page* vii

The Imprisonment of Obatala   I

Everyman   45

Woyengi   79

INTRODUCTION

Theatre in the Yoruba language is mostly a kind of opera, in which the songs are rehearsed, while the dialogue is improvised. In the late twenties and thirties this form was developed in the so-called African churches, the *Apostolic Church* and the *Seraphim and Cherubim*. The Bible stories and moralities performed by these church societies soon gave way to profane plays, social and political satires which were played by professional touring companies. Hubert Ogunde was the first and is still the most famous of these company directors, who are dramatist, composer, director and lead actor in one. For most of these plays no written text exists, and in a few cases, where students of drama took the trouble to transcribe live performances, the result is unrewarding. The texts do not stand up on their own, without the charm and the vitality of the performance.

Duro Ladipo was the first of these directors to whom the text mattered. For Ladipo is as much a poet as he is a musician. It was he who first explored the wealth of traditional Yoruba poetry in his plays. The *oriki* (praise names), the *ijala* (hunter's songs), the *iwi* (maskeraders' poetry), were all used and developed by him in plays like *Oba Koso, Oba Waja,* and *Oba Moro*. (See *Three Yoruba Plays* by Duro Ladipo, Mbari Publications, Ibadan, 1964).

Ladipo's plays are the first that have survived translation. *Oba Koso* has even been performed as a radio play in German on Radio Munich. (German adaptation by Klaus Stephan.)

There is no doubt that Obotunde Ijimere was directly inspired by Ladipo's plays. For a brief time, in fact, he was a member of Ladipo's theatre company but soon decided that acting was not really his line. He had been interested in writing for a long time and had tried his hand with English short stories in the Extra-Mural writer's workshops in Oshogbo. At the time, his tutor's advice to write in his native Yoruba tongue did not seem to click with him. But then the experience of *Oba Koso* suggested a new medium to him. He began to write plays for Ladipo's company. One of these plays, *Eda*, has already been performed by Ladipo with great success, not only in Nigeria but also in Germany, Austria, Switzerland and Belgium.

Ijimere's *Eda* is an adaptation of Hugo von Hofmanthal's *Everyman*. The basic theme has been retained, but the play has been *rethought* entirely in Yoruba. Thus the Christian mythology of Heaven and Hell has been replaced by the Yoruba concept of reincarnation. Everyman's greatest punishment would be to be 'thrown on the heaven of potsherds' – in other words, never to return to this earth again.

Unlike Ladipo, whose themes all come from oral tradition, Ijimere uses literary sources. *Woyengi* is based on an Ijaw tale, told by Gabriel Okara in *Black Orpheus* No 2. This play was first performed as a dance drama by students of the University of Ibadan Drama Department under the direction of Peggy Harper.

The major play of the three, however, *The Imprisonment of Obatala,* is once again based on a Yoruba myth. It seems likely that Ijimere was inspired to treat this theme by Susanne Wenger's repeated handling of the myth on her batiks and screen prints. (It was these, incidentally, that inspired J. P. Clark's poem of the same name.) *The Imprisonment of Obatala* is an ambitious play, which explores the philosophy of Yoruba *orisha* worship and tries to show the interplay of cosmic forces that are personified in the Yoruba imagination as *orisha* – supernatural beings, half human and historical, half divine and eternal.

A first performance of this play is being attempted by an international students group in Berlin.

Although written with the Duro Ladipo company in mind, these plays by Obotunde Ijimere seem adaptable to different groups and different techniques. While the language is largely based on traditional Yoruba imagery, as is Ladipo's, Ijimere explores new ground in his themes and ideas. Written with less direct experience of the stage and its needs than Ladipo's

Three Yoruba Plays, Ijimere's dramas may need rather more adaptation by individual directors. Nevertheless it is hoped that they will enrich the repertoire of Nigerian theatre in the future.

January 1966

U. B.

The Imprisonment of Obatala

CHARACTERS

OBATALA, *King of Ife and God of Creation*

YEMANJA, *his wife*

SHANGO, *King of Oyo and God of Thunder; Obatala's friend*

OYA, *Shango's wife*

ESHU, *God of fate*

OGUN, *God of war*

BABALAWO, *an oracle priest*

A FARMER

SERVANTS *of Shango*

WOMEN

THE IMPRISONMENT OF OBATALA

Scene I

The palace at Ife. YEMANJA *enters, carrying the new yam.*
OBATALA *is seated on his throne.*

YEMANJA (*singing*): Yam yam yam
   You are whiter than the cattle egret
   Whiter than teeth
   Whiter even than the gown of Obatala.
   Yam O yam O yam
   You have a cap of meat
   You have a gown of bitter leaf
   You have trousers of fish.
   Yam O yam O yam.
OBATALA: So the new yam has come again
   Whiter than teeth, whiter than salt,
   Whiter than eyeballs,
   Whiter than the beads in my crown.
   Yam:
   You have the power to turn a wise man into a fool.
   You cause the newly wedded wife to lose her manners.
   The modest man unbuttons his shirt, his eyes grow wide
   The new yam knows no difference between beggar and king
   Between the thief and the rich man, between man and God:
   You turn them all greedy alike.
YEMANJA: Blessed be the bald patch on the head of vulture.
   Had he not carried the sacrifice to heaven,
   How could we celebrate the new yam?
   We thank the owner of the sky for this year's rain:
   We thank the earth for bowing to the sky.

OBATALA: Ten years have passed, since we have settled
The quarrel between Heaven and Earth.
For the tenth year now, the earth has been pregnant
With the sperm of heaven,
Ten years, since Shango, owner of the palace,
Met me at Ife to plead with the earth.
How we rejoiced, when vulture rose to Heaven
Carrying Earth's sacrifice
And rain poured down once more
After the long drought.
Little we cared, that rivers of red mud
Washed away our houses, that the wind
Carried away the straw from our roofs
Scattering our belongings.
For the famine was over:
The yam sprouted from its mounds
Creeping up the sticks;
Corn cobs appeared
With rows and rows of gleaming teeth
And cassava, with a rough skin on its back,
Swelled up in the earth, red as camwood.

YEMANJA: Oh how we celebrated then!
Shango's belly got round with yam
Like that of a pregnant woman.
Nobody can eat like Shango!
When he has liver ache – he eats six pots of pounded yam
With bean soup.

OBATALA: This yam is no less creamy than last year's
Yet it sticks in my throat
Like yesterday's stale fufu.
The meat of the grass cutter,
Is every bit as sweet
And yet it goes gristly in my tongue
Like an old bull.

I wish Shango was here to celebrate with us!
Shango, my fiery friend, the owner of the palace,
Who spits fire from his mouth, who darts fire from his eyes.

YEMANJA: My Lord,
You keep longing for your fierce friend,
Because you know how to deal with him,
But we fear this man,
Who rides fire like a horse,
This man who has water,
Yet takes blood to wash.
He covers himself with the cloth of death
He shaves his children's heads with lightning!

OBATALA: A friend is precious like a child.
You cannot buy a friend in the market.
Two hundred needles do not amount to an axe.
One thousand stars do not shine like the sun.
The loyalty of two thousand servants
Does not compensate for the absence of a friend.
A friend's temper cannot be so foul —
That we should cease to love him.
His actions cannot be so crooked —
That we should cease to respect him.
His face cannot be so ugly —
That we should cease to admire him.
See that my horse is saddled. Prepare my clothes,
And food for seven days.
Tomorrow, before my praise names sound on the Igbin
    drum
I must be on my way.

YEMANJA: My husband:
Anybody who waits for the buffalo waits for death!
Anybody who waits for the elephant waits for death!
Do not provoke the god of fate with this rash trip.
The Kingdom of Oyo is harsh.

The heat has burnt the forest into ashes.
The baobab alone survived the scorching sun.
The harmattan
Will whiten your skin and redden your eyes.
Shango may be your friend,
But he is surrounded by ruffians,
By warriors who kill the owner of the house
And paint the hearth with his blood.
They kill on the left, they kill on the right,
And they will not welcome you,
Bringer of peace.

OBATALA: Yemanja, my wife,
Owner of brass and parrot's feathers,
Your skin is black like velvet,
The palms of your hand are soft like liver,
Your teeth are white like corn.
You have the wisdom of elders
And the knowledge of the oracle.
Yet my desire is stronger than your wisdom
And my impatience is greater than your knowledge.
Yemanja, my wife.
Owner of brass and parrot's feathers,
I have decided on this trip.
And yet;
To show respect to your head
I will do this:
Tonight, when the oil lamps
Have been extinguished on the market
And the owner of the house turns over heavily
On his side,
His belly bloated with the evening meal,
Then I will call the father of secrets
To hear what awaits me on this trip.
His advice I will follow,

All necessary sacrifices and concoctions I will make.
Yet even if his prophecy is death:
My longing will be stronger than his wisdom
And my desire stronger than his knowledge.

CURTAIN

OBATALA *is consulting the* BABALAWO. *The room is dimly lit. The* BABALAWO *throws the palm-nuts and chants the ritual verse:*

BABALAWO: This is the oracle of the hunter
Who followed the antelope
To the forest of Onikorogbo.
He was told to sacrifice
In order to avoid his death.
He was told to sacrifice eggs,
All the eggs in his house.
The hunter refused to sacrifice.
He followed the antelope
In the forest of Onikorogbo.
His pregnant wife
Had demanded its skin to lie on,
So that she would bear a beautiful child.
But the antelope stepped out like a prince
Shaking the grass like bells.
The hunter said: Antelope with the beautiful neck
You are worth more than twenty slaves,
You are worth more than thirty servants!
The hunter aimed at the white patch
Round the antelope's cunt.
But the antelope said: Zeeeeeeduuuu —
And the antelope escaped.
The hunter wandered through the forest of Onikorogbo
But all the animals had vanished.

When he wanted to return home —
He met death.
For a while they hunted together.
At last they found two eggs.
The hunter wanted to share them —
But death refused.
The hunter went home lonely.
Soon after that famine came.
The hunter cooked the eggs
And cooked them for his children.
Then death arrived and said:
I have come for my share,
There is famine in heaven.
The hunter said: Alas,
I tried to shoot the white patch of the antelope
I tried to extinguish its sparkling eye.
But I hit the iroko tree
I had to eat the eggs with my children.
Then death killed the hunter and his children.

OBATALA: Father of secrets, your nuts portend evil,
You prophecy is death.
But know that my desire is greater than your knowledge,
That my eagerness is greater than your wisdom.
Even if death is unavoidable
I am determined to behold the fire
That is sparkling in Shango's eyes.
Throw your nuts again and ask
What sacrifices may buy off
The greedy hands of death.

BABALAWO: Obatala,
Who turns blood into children!
Obatala, who can turn a single man into two hundred!
Divine craftsman, second only to the owner of heaven:
You have an account to settle with the God of fate.

Olodumare, the immovable rock, who never dies,
Olodumare, the eye of heaven, that does not grow any
    grass,
Olodumare, the owner of the sun, the sky and the earth,
Appointed you his craftsman
To mould the features of man.
Obatala who turns blood into children,
You who make nose and eyes,
You who make penis and vagina,
You betrayed the trust of Olodumare.
You drank the milky wine of the palm
Cool and sizzling it was in the morning,
Fermenting in the calabash.
Its sweet foam overflowed
Like the eyes of a woman in love.
You refreshed yourself in the morning
But by evening time your hands were unsteady,
Your senses were dull, your fingertips numbed.
And then,
You made the blind man who cannot see
The whiteness of the cattle egret,
Nor the blackness of the hornbill,
Nor the redness of the cuckal.
You made the red-eyed albino
Who is frightened of the sun,
Whose skin is sore like the leper's.
You made the hunchback,
Laughing stock of children,
Shunned by women,
A living calabash of medicine.
You must pay for your sins:
As soon as you leave this sacred city,
Eshu will be waiting for you behind the iroko tree,
He will be hidden in anthills,

You will meet him on the road and in the bush,
In the savanna and in the farm.

OBATALA: Father of secrets:
Praised be Olodumare the Almighty:
You do not know his father
You do not know his mother
The liars are only lying.
Whatever fate awaits me,
I will accept.
Whatever suffering Eshu has thought up for me
I will suffer!
Before my praise names sound on the Igbin drum to-
morrow
I will set out to behold
The fire in the eyes of my friend.

BABALAWO: This was the prophecy for the king of Awe
Who conquered his foes through patience:
The river abuses the rock —
The rock keeps quiet.
The river attacks the rock —
The rock does not fight back.
The river swallows the rock —
The rock holds still.
But when the dry season comes
The river is lost in the sand
His fishes turn white bellies to heaven,
But the rock remains immobile
Where God had planted it.
Shango may thrive in war,
Orunmila may thrive through wisdom,
But you will thrive in suffering.
      The BABALAWO *goes out.*

OBATALA: Yemanja, my wife!
Yemanja,

Owner of brass and parrot's feathers.
    YEMANJA *enters*.
The father of secrets has spoken.
The journey I will undertake on foot.
Prepare my sleeping cloth of spotless white
Bring me my calabash and walking-stick.
Disguised as a mendicant priest
I will beg my way to Oyo.
Unprotected will I face the tricks of Eshu,
Behind the iroko tree will I expect him,
And in the anthill.
What Olodumare has destined for me, I will suffer.
But in the end, I will set eyes on Shango,
I will see the fire in his eyes, the fire in his mouth.
Shango, who rides fire like a horse,
Shango who seizes his neighbour's roof
To cover his own house:
Shango who lends out money
And forgets to claim it back.
    WOMEN *of the household have entered during the speech.*
    YEMANJA *is now getting his cloth and calabash and walking-*
    stick. She hands them to OBATALA, *while the women sing*
    his praises.
WOMEN: Obatala, who turns blood into children.
You stand by your children and let them succeed.
You cause them to laugh – and they laugh.
Obatala who turns blood into children.
We shall dance to your sixteen drums.
To eight drums we dance erect,
Twisting our shoulders.
To eight drums we dance bending down,
Shaking our hips,
Obatala, the patient one,
Go well and come well,

Obatala, the silent one,
Obatala who turns blood into children,
We shall wait for you,
Dancing to your sixteen drums.

CURTAIN

In the forest. ESHU *sits under a tree with a jar of palm oil.*
   OBATALA *enters, singing.*

OBATALA: A friend is as precious as a child.
   You cannot buy a friend on the market.
   His arms cannot be so thin —
   That you should rub a stranger's arm with camwood.
   His buttocks cannot be so flat —
   That you should tie the beads round a stranger's waist.
   His eyes cannot be so ugly —
   That you should paint a stranger's eyes with antimony.
ESHU: Wanderer in the forest!
   A single hand cannot lift the load on the head.
   The little hand of the child cannot reach the shelf under the
      roof;
   The large hand of the adult cannot enter the narrow neck of
      the calabash.
   The stranger of today could be the friend of tomorrow.
   Wanderer in the forest:
   Help me to lift my load on my head.
OBATALA: Stranger by the wayside,
   Your words are sweet,
   But your eyes are evil.
   Yet what you ask of me
   No man can ever refuse:
   For a single hand
   Cannot lift the load on one's head.
      As he helps to lift the pot on ESHU's *head,* ESHU *quickly*

pours the contents over OBATALA's *head and jumps aside.*

ESHU (*laughs*): Kindness has never killed anybody,
  But it gives one a lot of troubles.
      He runs off. OBATALA *makes to strike* ESHU, *but quickly remembers the prophecy. His arm drops and he stands immobile. He speaks slowly as if to himself.*

OBATALA: Eshu confuser of men:
  When he is angry, he hits a stone until it bleeds.
  When he is angry he sits on the skin of an ant.
  When he is angry he weeps tears of blood.
      The lights go out. When the scene lights up a minute later, the forest has changed into savanna studded with red termite hills. To the left of the stage a FARMER *is digging the ground. On the right* OBATALA *rests in the shade.*
  Your soil is red, my friend, and rich.
  Tomorrow even the bits of cassava
  Idly thrown away by careless eaters
  Will swell in the ground and
  Turn red like camwood.

FARMER: Blessed we are with the soil
  And cursed with neighbours.
  Today our soil produces yam
  Too big for our stomachs,
  But tomorrow even
  Shango's greedy soldiers
  May plant the fire on our roofs.
  And carry away the whitest of our yams
  And the blackest of our women.

OBATALA: Your sad tale is good news to me:
  Am I so near then, to the kingdom of Oyo?

FARMER: Hardly a day's trip from here,
  And you will meet his fiery soldiers
  Guarding the boundary.

Beware of their anger:
They are quick to use iron and brass
Before they ask questions;
They are quick to kill
Before you can answer.

    ESHU *passes between them. He wears a dress and cap which are*
    red on one side and black on the other.

ESHU (*sings*): The hunter thinks the monkey is not wise
The monkey *is* wise
But he has his own logic.

FARMER: Who was that cheeky fellow dressed in red?
His presence made me feel cold in the heart:
He portends evil.

OBATALA: Cheeky he was indeed
And I agree with you
That his uncanny presence
May likely mean disaster.
But was he dressed in red?
Surely his dress was black!

FARMER: Are you trying to provoke me?
Have I not eyes in my head?
My eyes like birds
Are wont to fly over two hundred trees.
I see the weaver bird hiding
In the silk cotton tree.
The antelope stiffening in the grass
Cannot elude me.
My gun has hit the hawk
When it stands in the centre of the sky
Quivering
Ready to pounce on my chicken.
That man – stranger – wore red!

OBATALA: I am a man of peace.
Far be it from me to quarrel with a stranger.

Yet I could swear by the iron that digs the bleeding soil
That this man's dress was black!

> *The* FARMER *makes a move to strike* OBATALA *in anger:*
> *but at the very moment* ESHU *passes again from the other*
> *direction – now his red side faces* OBATALA *and black side*
> *faces the* FARMER.

ESHU (*sings*): The hunter thinks the monkey is not wise,
The monkey *is* wise:
But he has his own logic.

FARMER: My God – am I dreaming?
My head has been confused.
The sun has burned too long on the back of my head
My eyes have stared too long at the blood-red soil:
They have begun to see red everywhere.
Forgive me, stranger, you were right.
This fellow's dress was black indeed.

OBATALA: What madness is this?
This man sang the same song
And his presence was uncanny as before.
Yet I swear by the iron of your hoe
That digs the bleeding soil
That this was not the same fellow
We have been seeing twice.
For the first, I swear, was wearing black,
While the second, I know it, was certainly red!

FARMER: Stranger: will you confuse my senses?
Are you trying to work spells on me?
I will not suffer your witchcraft!

> *The* FARMER *strikes* OBATALA. *For a moment* OBATALA
> *tries to defend himself – then suddenly he lets his arms drop*
> *and allows himself to be beaten to the ground. The* FARMER
> *goes off furiously.*

OBATALA (*sitting on the ground, speaks slowly, as if to himself*):
Eshu confuser of men!

The newly wedded wife sacrificed to Eshu;
She thought he would not confuse her head,
Until one day she stole the sacrifice from the altar!
The newly installed queen sacrificed to Eshu;
She thought he would not confuse her head,
Until one morning she walked naked in the market.

The stage darkens. When it lights up a moment later, the scene is a very open savanna country.

OBATALA: Only the baobab has here survived.
The fierceness of the burning sun.
The harmattan has turned my skin white;
Dust has reddened my eyes and split my lips
Surely this must be the country of Shango.
Today I shall behold him
Who rides fire like a horse.
I shall set eyes on the death
That drops *to to to*
Like dark indigo from the drying cloth.

Shango's horse, loose, runs on to the stage.

Good omen, I am nearer than I thought.
This horse can only be Shango's.
Who else could dare to mount
This creature blacker than the hornbill,
Quicker than fire, trembling like water.
No other horse could be as richly decked
With brass and purple, with coloured leather
Silver reins and parrot's feathers.
Let me seize the fugitive and bring him to my friend.

As OBATALA *seizes the horse Shango's* SERVANTS *enter, shouting.*

SERVANTS: Look at the thief!
His eyes were greedy for brass and silver
He coveted bright embroidery
Brighter than weaver birds

Glistening like humming birds.
Oh what a fool to steal a horse he dare not mount!
In jail he may consider his folly.

OBATALA: My friends, you know not who I am:
  If Shango hears my name
  His eyes will shine like suns
  His mouth will speak . . . the . . .

  OBATALA *remembers the prophecy. He stutters and falls into*
  silence.

SERVANT: Many words do not fill a basket.
  The man who has planted a hundred yams
  And boasts of two hundred
  Will have to eat his lies when the yam is finished.
  Take him to prison!

  As they bind his hands on his back, OBATALA *stands quietly*
  and says slowly, more to himself than to the servants:

OBATALA: Eshu confuser of men!
  When he is angry he hits a stone until it bleeds.
  Having thrown a stone today – he kills a bird of yesterday.

CURTAIN

SHANGO'S *palace.* SHANGO *sits in state as the* OLORIS *(his wives) sing his praises.*

OLORIS: The dog follows its master
  Though it does not know where he is going.
  The sheep stays in the house of its master
  It does not know that he will kill it in the end.
  We adore Shango, the owner of the palace,
  Though we do not know his intentions.
  It is not easy to live in Shango's company.
  Crab's feet are confusion
  The parrot's feet are crooked.
  When the crab leaves its hole
  We cannot guess the direction it is taking.
  Shango went to Ibadan and arrived in Ilorin.
    A SERVANT *enters.*
SERVANT. My Lord,
  Anybody who waits for the elephant waits for death!
  Anybody who waits for the buffalo waits for death!
  This man's foolishness betrays his old age.
  His rashness belied his years.
  He was caught stealing your war horse
  Bedecked with brass and parrot's feathers
  On the way to Igbeti.
SANGO (*angry – but not yet recognizing* OBATALA): My horse
  – dearest of my possessions.
  Swifter than the arrows of the Tapas,
  Lighter than the hawk quivering in the sky.

His haunches round like a woman's buttocks,
He is black like velvet; only the foam is white
That gathers round his mouth
Like palm wine overflowing its calabash.
He is vain but obedient like a new wife,
Submissive to my touch, but prepared
To throw any other rider in the dust.
Excitement ripples on his flank
When I approach. His black eyeballs gleam
Like those of a dancer possessed.
The man who was fool enough to lay hands on him
Does not deserve to live.

OBATALA: Shango who rides fire like a horse.
Draped in the cloth of death.
Shango who kills money with a big stick.
Shango who strikes the one who is stupid,
Shango who wrinkles his nose and the liar runs off.
It is true, ten years have passed,
Since we dispatched the vulture to heaven:
Ten years since vulture staggered
Under the weight of Earth's sacrifice.
Ten years since the two of us
Have shared the new yam that is whiter
Than the eyes of a woman in love.
And yet:
The taste of friendship lingers in the mouth
Like bitter kola nut.
Like cassava carelessly thrown on the rubbish dump
Will sprout
Even neglected friendship will not die.
Have you forgotten those days of famine
When even Ogun, who bathes in blood,
Was forced to turn peace-maker
And for once had to join us in pleading

With mother earth to submit to the sky?
Have you forgotten that first rain,
When the red laterite soil
Was washed away in torrential rivers of blood,
When we were happy, even though the roofs
Scattered in the air like a rain of straw
And the palace walls fell with sudden thud
And men and goats were drifting off in the whirl?
Have you forgotten that first yam
We dug from the earth, as big
As a woman's thigh?
And the red cassava with rough skin
On its back?
Do you forget Yemanja pounding
That first new yam,
Her breasts dancing like hungry dogs?

SHANGO: Oh horror!
Is it you, Obatala, who turns blood into children?
Is it you, Obatala the father of laughter?
Could I ever forget the day we danced to your sixteen
    drums?
Is it possible that the wisest of all
Should have become the most foolish?
And the purest, the most foul?
Oh horror, the father of laughter,
Who rides the hunchback, has turned
A common thief.
Have your fingers become long, like
Those of the red monkey
Who says: I am not a thief,
I only take what I want in the presence of the farmer.
Have you become greedy for cowries and brass
Like the he-goat on heat trying to mount his mother?
Are you lusting for silver and parrot's feathers

Like the wild pig whose long rubbery nose
Twists and sniffs about the undergrowth
Following the slimy cunt of his mate?
Is it possible,
You have become a common thief,
Like one running naked through the night
His body silky with red oil
To slip through grabbing hands?
Did you think that the owner of heaven
Would cover your secret?
Fool!
Did you think you could shit on the road
And not find flies on your return?
TAKE HIM AWAY!
> OBATALA *is about to flare up in defence when he suddenly*
> *remembers the prophecy, and falls silent.*

OYA: My Lord, Shango,
Who rides fire like a horse!
The man who thinks of nothing but the irritation of the itch
Could easily scratch himself to the bone!
Beware of rashness!
The knife that thinks it is only destroying an old sheath
Is in fact destroying its own house!

SHANGO: Will you ask the husband to be patient
When his wife has been raped?
Shall fire stop burning
Because it is friendly with wood?
It is easier to kill the antelope in the bush
Than to sacrifice the dog in your own house.
It is easier to forgive one's enemy
Than to forgive one's friend!
Take him to prison and out of my sight!

OYA (*comforting* OBATALA): You think the worm is dancing,
But that is merely the way it walks.

You think Shango is fighting you,
But that is merely the way he is.
OBATALA (*as they seize him*): Eshu confuser of men!
Having thrown a stone yesterday
You kill a bird today.
You turn right into wrong, wrong into right.
Shango —
I have longed to see the fire in your eyes,
And I left the steaming dampness of my forests
The black-leaved Iroko tree
And the white-stemmed silk cotton trees.
I came into your scorched savanna
Where the baobab alone has survived the burning sun
Stretching his leprous fingers against the milky sky.
The red-tailed parrot and the shimmering honey bird
Shun this shadeless country; only the cattle egret
Rides on your long-horned bull
And the red kite lamely flaps his wings
Over the burning bush, ready for the rat
That flees the fire.
Shango —
How I had longed for this day!
But Eshu the weaver of fate
Has confused the threads.
Now I must wait
For him to disentangle them himself.
Eshu who turns right into wrong;
Wrong into right.
    The SERVANTS *lead* OBATALA *away.*
SHANGO: It must have been the wisdom of his elders
That prevented Obatala from being a fool.
What madness to steal a horse he cannot ride
Like an impotent old chief
Who marries a moist young wife

And hides the shrivelled fruit
Between his legs.
Oh, had he tried to mount
This quivering black flame
He would have shook him off
Even quicker than the frustrated wife
Got rid of her limp husband
Who lacked the tool
To make her bleed and sweat.

OYA: My Lord, owner of the palace,
The taste of friendship lingers in the mouth
Like a bitter kola nut.
Have you forgotten the sacred city of Ife
Steaming with the blood of sacrifices
In the temples of the four hundred and one gods?
Have you forgotten the trembling voice
Of the praise singer, the monotonous chant
Of the father of secrets, the piercing ring
Of the iron gong of the town crier
As you entered the town?
The virgins had painted themselves with camwood
And were dancing in your honour.
The coral beads shone bright in their hair,
Their waist beads gave their narrow hips
A semblance of maturity; their breasts
Were almost too small to dance to the rhythm of the drums
Obatala's wives were sweating in the back yard
Pounding the heavy yams; the pestles
Sounded darkly in the mortars
Like Obatala's sixteen Igbin drums.
The hunter brought the long-horned antelope
Its body hanging limp from his shoulder.
Its tail had fallen loosely aside
Exposing the cold vagina, and its thin legs

That once made the grass ring like bells
Were dangling stiffly on his back.
The calabashes were buzzing with palm wine
And the white fermenting foam
Slowly crept down their sides
Like the male seed, gently backflowing
Down a woman's thigh.
My Lord,
I know you strike before you ask,
And you kill before a man can answer!
But is it possible you forgot your friend?
The dancer possessed by his god is insensitive to pain
He feels not the knife in his chest
Or the iron thrust through his tongue —
Yet he will wake up bleeding.

SHANGO: Oya my wife,
Tempt me no more.
When thunder strikes
It kills friends and enemies alike.
Do you want me to eat my own words?
Or like a dog lap up my own vomit?
If I should wake up bleeding tomorrow
Let me die of it.
The friend who betrayed me
Shall never be forgiven.
If my right hand is leprous
Let it rot off and fall.
Oya my wife,
No other person can have
Tongue or lips
To talk to me like you.
Yet I will forgive you
Even this provocation
For there is no other woman

In whose eye I like to see my own reflection.
No other woman has a neck as long or hips as black as you.
  Sudden heavy drum-rolls; shots are heard; shouts and screaming
  women.
OYA: My Lord,
Even now the imprisonment of Obatala spells disaster.
The bringer of peace, the father of laughter is in jail,
You have unleashed Ogun, who bathes in blood.
Even now his reign begins:
He kills suddenly in the house and suddenly in the field.
He kills the child with the iron with which it plays.
Ogun kills the owner of the slaves and the slaves as well.
He kills the owner of the house and paints the hearth with
  his blood!
SHANGO: Obatala has made women of us all.
The leopard cannot live on grass!
Should the lion feast on bitter leaf?
Now we shall discover the ones
With watery bellies
And soft knees,
The ones whose mouths are toothless
Like tortoise,
Whose feet are soft padded
Like hares.
Many now will be dumb
Like fish spawning with fear in the water
They will stiffen like antelopes in the grass
Or turn yellow like chameleons
Sitting on corn cobs.
Bring me my sword!
I'll drive the attackers back into their town.
Within three days
The stench of corpses in their market-place
Will haunt the survivors in the bush!

Ogun shall have his due today.
We shall not be stingy with our sacrifices:
The curdling blood shall form black swamps
Reeking by the wayside
And the vulture at last shall be rewarded:
He will forget the bald patch on his head
As he will stalk with feathered feet
Through intestines
While he will feast on the eyes of fallen warriors.

During his speech the war cries and shots have continued behind the scene. Armed soldiers have crowded around him ready to go to war. At the end he is handed his sword and leads them off to war.

CURTAIN

SHANGO's *palace.* WOMEN *enter, singing* OGUN's *praises.*

WOMEN: Ogun is not like pounded yam,
  Do you think you can knead him in your hand
  And eat of him until you are satisfied?
  Ogun is not like maize gruel:
  Do you think you can drink him
  Until the calabash is drained?
  Ogun is not something you can carry in one hand:
  Do you think you can put him in your cap
  And walk away with him?
  Ogun kills in the dead of night
  And during the heat of the day.
  When Ogun wants to kill
  He does not care whether it rains or the sun shines.
  He kills the rat in its hole
  The squirrel on the tree
  And the eagle in the middle of the sky.
  The leopard claws the earth,
  Blood oozes from his nostrils,
  His eyes stare white towards the sky
  When he is hit by Ogun.
  The elephant roars like the *kakaki* trumpet
  His trunk threatens to tear the sky
  Like an old rag.
  But when he is struck by Ogun,
  His tree-trunk legs snap like broomsticks,
  And his weight comes thundering down

As camwood and iroko are crushed
Under his load.
And the forest dove shrieks and flutters in the sky
When its nest hits the ground with the iroko
And the yolks of its eggs are scattered.

OGUN *enters, dancing.*

WOMEN: The lion never allows anybody to play with his cub.
Ogun will never allow his child to be punished.
Ogun, do not reject me!
Does the woman who spins ever reject the spindle?
Does the woman who dyes ever reject the cloth?
Does the eye that sees ever reject a sight?
Ogun, do not reject me.

OGUN *continues his dance, and finally sits down exhausted on the right.*

OGUN: Shango is a king after my own heart.
For ten years now, he has not let the iron rest!
He has raided both Tapa and Borgu,
Idahomi and Kabba.
Wherever he goes,
He leaves behind crumbling walls
And black ashes, and the blood of virgins
Raped by his greedy men, mingles
With the blood of the slain.

OYA: This city has been filled with slaves
And this palace with women:
With yellow skins or long necks,
With black buttocks or fat thighs
With breasts like mangoes
Or palms soft like liver —
They all succumbed to the owner of the palace.
Their bodies grow heavy with the king's fruit:
But alas a curse has fallen on this city:
Some women die in childbirth; they bleed

Until their body is drained and dry.
Or else the fruit rots in their womb
Before it sees the light of day.
For sometime now, the swelling belly
And the pendulous heavy breasts, a woman's pride,
Seem like a death sentence.
The women fear the king, when he returns
For a brief spell from the war
His ankles crusted with blood
His body sweaty and caked with red earth.
The women tremble when he calls them to his mat
And he must force their thighs asunder
And the heat of lust in their bodies
Mingles with the cold sweat of fear.
A curse has fallen on Oyo.
The corn on its stalk is worm-eaten
And hollow like an old honeycomb;
The yam in the earth is dry and stringy like
Palm wood.
I fear that we are paying now
For the king's injustice.
No one can maltreat the father of laughter
With impunity. Creation comes to a standstill
When he who turns blood into children
Is lingering in jail.
OGUN (*jumping up in anger*): Let us not hear of him.
We had his peace too long!
The iron rusted in the smithy
And the smith grew rings round his waist.
I had grown tired of the blood of dogs
Offered as substitute by men
Who had grown soft and fat like eunuchs.
The king of laughter had his time
Now let me quench my thirst!

Bata drums are heard behind the scene and cries of Kabiyesi O !
Then SHANGO *enters triumphantly.*

WOMEN: Shango walks alone, but he enters the town like a
swarm of locusts.
When Shango leaves a town
The blazing houses shine brighter than suns,
And weary warriors bathe in their own blood.
Heads and limbs are cheaper than last year's yam
And the girls lie exhausted
With the snail bleeding between their legs.

OYA: My Lord,
Welcome in your city and your palace.
You return like a hero.
Fire in your eyes, fire in your mouth, fire on the roofs.
The blood has hardly dried on your limbs
And you shine like the priest
Whose ritual camwood paint
Gleams before the altar.
You have brought more wealth to the city
Your servants stagger under the weight of cowries
And indigo cloth. Embroidered gowns and brass rings
Horses, slaves and long-necked women you bring.
Alas: wealth has become useless in Oyo.
Ten thousand cowries cannot buy one yam.
Your town, its soil, and people have been cursed!
I pray, Lord,
Send for the father of secrets,
That he may tell us,
How to break the spell.

SHANGO: No one has tongue and lips
To speak to me like you
And yet I must forgive you:
No other woman ever was as black as you
Your shiny skin reflects the redness of my cloth

Softer than liver
Is the touch of your hand.
So let it be:
Call for the father of secrets
That he may tell us how to break the spell.

OGUN: Shango, king after my own heart,
Who rides fire like a horse
Who rides lightning like a woman:
Do not listen to the advice of women!
Their thoughts are hidden
Like the body of tortoise.
And remember:
The fathers of our secrets have been known
To throw their nuts to please their customers.

BABALAWO *enters.*

SHANGO: Father of secrets
Throw your palm nuts,
Draw your secret symbols into flour
And chant your sacred verse
To let us know:
Why our children die and why crops fail!
Teach us the sacrifice and spells,
Concoctions, prayers and actions
That may break the curse.

The BABALAWO *throws his nuts and draws in the flour. Then
he chants:*

BABALAWO (*chanting*): Anybody who looks down
Will surely see his nose.
But the man who strikes before he asks
Who kills before he is answered
Is like a blind man
To whom the cattle egret is as black as the hornbill.
Orunmila tells the story of a dog
Who was interlocked with his mate

When they made love.
Then he decided to leave her for another bitch
And he cut off his penis to break loose.
Then he came to Orunmila and asked:
Why can't I have any children?
But no sacrifice could cure him.
No one can cut off a friend
Without hurting himself.
Have you drunk so much blood
That you washed away
The taste of bitter kola nut?
Have you seen so much blood
That you see nothing but red?
Can you see the whiteness of the gown
Of the old man who suffers in silence?
Do you expect your children to thrive
And your crops to ripen
When the father of laughter is imprisoned?
Do you expect your women to deliver
When he who turns blood into children
When he who make eyes and makes nose
Is living on water and cold maize pap?
Anyone who looks down
Will surely see his nose.
But the one who strikes before he asks
And kills before he is answered
Is as blind as the bat in daylight.

SHANGO: Oh father of secrets,
I have been like the performing priest
Who thrusts knives into his body
Insensitive to pain in his dance.
Now I have woken after the dance – bleeding.
I was like the man
Who carried water in a basket.

I captured women
Red like antelopes or black
Like indigo.
But my seed was poison injected between their thighs;
They swelled up horribly and died.
The iron I had dipped in blood
Was like poisoned arrows thrust into the soil
And the yam it dug up
Was shrivelled up like an abortion.
I have cursed myself and my town
Because I imprisoned the creator.
Go and release the father of laughter
Let us ask forgiveness of him
Who turns blood into children.

WOMEN: Obatala is silent, he is not angry.
He sits in silence to pass judgement.
He sees you, even when he is not looking.
He may be in a far place – but his eyes are on the town.
We dance to your sixteen drums, jingindiringin,
To eight drums we dance erect
With twisting shoulders,
To eight drums we dance bending down
With shaking buttocks.
Munusi Munusi Munusi,
We dance to your sixteen drums, jingindiringin.

> OBATALA, *in an immaculate white gown, is carried in shoulder high by* SERVANTS.

SHANGO: Oh father of laughter!
I was like the patient who was cured
And beat his doctor.
I was foolish like the knife
That destroys its own sheath.
Father:
Many words do not fill a basket.

The most beautiful speech
Falls like water through wickerwork
Oh father of laughter
Try to forgive the injustice done to you.
OBATALA: He who admits his fault
   Will not be kept kneeling for long.
   When death is not ready to receive somebody
   He will send him a doctor at the right time.
   So here I am at last
   Beholding the fire in your eyes again.
   Shango
   My suffering was not your doing.
   I had an account to settle
   With the God of fate.
   The owner of heaven has not forgiven me
   For in my drunkenness
   I had made the Albino
   Whose bleached skin is sore like the lepers,
   I had made the hunchback
   To whom women close their thighs
   And the blind man
   Who is helpless like a bat in sunlight.
   Eshu, confuser of men,
   Has brought my suffering about.
   Throwing a stone today
   He killed a bird yesterday;
   But let us now rejoice:
   The taste of friendship lingers in the mouth
   Like bitter kola nut.
   Friendship like lost virginity
   Can never be undone.
   True friendship never takes offence:
   I asked you to be patient,
   You were wildly impatient

And I loved you for it.
I asked you to be peaceful,
You steeped your arms in blood
But I still loved you for it.

OYA leads in a chorus of women. They are bringing in the new yam. It has been pounded and lies in white balls in the flat calabashes they carry. They dance and sing.

OYA: Yam, yam, yam,
You are whiter than the cattle egret,
Whiter than teeth
Whiter even than the gown of Obatala.
Yam O yam O yam.
You have a cap of meat
You have a gown of bitter leaf
You have trousers of fish.
Yam, O yam, O yam.

OGUN: Father of laughter
Your reign has begun.
Once more you have come to us
To turn blood into children.
I bow to the master craftsman
Who moulds the red clay
Who makes eyes and makes nose.
The child in the womb will live again:
Your shielding hand once more
Blesses our women.
I shall retire from your dazzling presence,
Your immaculate whiteness
Drives me back into the darkness of my forest.
Now the blood will dry on swords and arrows
The elders forging weapons in the smithy
Will grow fat.
The river of blood that fed me has dried up.
I will have to be satisfied with a trickle

That flows from circumcisions and tribal
Markings.
Grudgingly, I shall retire to my forest,
I will be comforted by the wisdom of the red monkey
And by the games of the Colobus.
I shall be amused by the baboon
Who has eyeballs to seduce a woman,
The baboon who kills lice with a black hand.
I shall face the wild buffalo
Who makes the hunter promise
Never to hunt again.
When he sees him in the bush the hunter cries:
I only borrowed the gun!
I will face the wild pig
That has matchets in its mouth;
When it points its tail towards heaven
The hunter has water in his belly.
I will meet the elephant
Who can pull down two palm-trees
With his single hand
If he had two hands, he would tear the heavens
Like an old rag!
I will return to the silent darkness of my forest.
Death and creation
Cannot live too close together.
Yet remember: They cannot live too far apart either.
The iron you despise
The iron you wish to imprison
It is the same iron
Used to carve your sacred images.
The iron makes the mahogany weep
When it chisels out the bulging eyes
That stare in a trance.
The iron makes the mahogany groan

When it moulds the mango breasts
Heavy and pendulous, as if with milk.
The iron makes the mahogany scream
When it cuts the parallel incisions of the mouth
And the triangular ornament of the pubis.
Father of laughter:
I yield to you now;
But the iron that serves you
Will one day shout for blood!

    OGUN *goes out with his attendants.*

SHANGO: This glorious day shall never be forgotten.
Let the praises of Obatala split the membranes of the dundun
    drum!
Let the praises of Obatala bathe the bata drummers in
    sweat.
Let the dark pounding of the Igbin drum mingle
With the pounding of the new yam.
Let my wives not rest:
Let their breasts leap like hungry dogs.
Let the father of laughter share the maize beer of the
    women:
But for the rest of us, bring the sizzling palm wine.
It is humming in the calabashes like a swarm of bees.
It froths like my war-horse on its bit
And its gentle coolness shall turn our eyes
And make us lovable to our wives at night.
Nothing shall remind us today of the blood of battle,
Unless it be the red palm oil that drenches
The whiteness of the yam.
The killing must end today:
Only the long-horned antelope
Will feel the iron in its chest today,
Its eyes will stiffen into glass
And its cunt will be cold like fish.

When the hunter staggers under its weight to the feast
The virgins shall dance for the father of laughter
The blue segy beads shall make their necks look longer.
The black waistbeads shall give them a semblance
Of maturity.
A new and happy time
Has begun for our kingdom.
Our soil is once more giving birth
To yams, cassava and corn.
Everywhere the black pots now are squatting
And the red fire licks their bottom.
The father of laughter is once more
Protecting our women.
Now the young bride will leave her father's house
Fearlessly,
Pretending only to weep.
And she will shout wildly:
Let me have seven times two hundred children!
And the snail, sacred to Obatala,
Will be offered at the altar of the creator
By the maidens; and when the knife cuts its head
And the sap is spilled, there will be shrieks of joy.

WOMEN: Obatala is patient – he is not angry.
He rests in the sky like a swarm of bees.
He rides on the hunchbacks:
He stretches out his right hand,
He stretches out his left hand.
Those who are rich owe their property to him.
Those who are poor owe their property to him.
Obatala, the silent one:
Whenever you take from the rich,
Come and give it to me.
Obatala who turns blood into children.
I have only one cloth to dye with blue indigo.

I have only one headtie to dye with red camwood.
But I know you keep twenty, thirty children for me
Whom I shall bear.
BABALAWO: I am blessing two not one,
This was prophesied to the sea lily
That reaches down into the mud, the origin of creation.
The time of creation has come.

CURTAIN

ESHU *stands alone on the stage. He is wearing his black and red gown.*

ESHU: Now they are happy.
   Obatala rests in the sky like a swarm of bees.
   He watches the world in silence
   Ogun has retired to the dark forest of Ekiti.
   Idly he watches woodcock and tree creeper.
   He listens to the gossip of the weaver birds
   And the prophecies of the owl.
   He understands the wisdom of the bombill
   And the humour of the cookcal.
   In Oyo the celebrants are sleeping.
   The yam is heavy in their bellies
   The wine is still fermenting in their heads
   Their lust is overpowered by their sleep.
   Their wives are snoring untouched, unhurt
   And undelighted, beside them on the mat.
   They will wake up to times of plenty:
   For years to come
   The earth will never fail them;
   The palm-tree will not cease to bleed
   For them with oil and wine.
   Their women will conceive
   As soon as they have weaned the other child.
   These are the times for the weavers,
   The goldsmiths and drummers and praise singers
   To grow fat on the vanity of women.

Little do they remember the rule of Ogun.
The stench of smouldering houses
And of rotting bodies has left their noses;
Red to them means oil, not blood.
Coldness to them is fish, not corpse.
Stench to them is merely shit, not rotting death.
Yet in serving Obatala, the father of laughter,
In worshipping the father of peace
They still use iron.
Obatala's children must suffer the iron
On their cheeks and penises
As soon as they can walk.
The goat offered to the father of laughter
Suffer Ogun's iron on its throat.
The child that Obatala moulds in the womb
Is begot and born with blood.
Ogun's iron is merely sleeping,
For a while it is satisfied
With a mere trickle of blood.
Ogun is like the baby lizard
Whose head is camouflaged with the female green;
But when the penis stiffens between his scaly legs
His true red colour will blaze out on his head
Proving battle; and his deadly tail will be ready
To slash his opponent's belly.
The time will come when the owner of Heaven
Will send me back to confuse the heads of men.
Then Ogun will burst out of his forest
To cool his parched throat with blood.
Then the father of laughter will be driven from the city.
And the rule of iron returns.
For if Obatala is the right arm of the owner of Heaven
Ogun is his left arm.
If Obatala's love is the right eye of the owner of the sun,

Ogun's iron is his left eye.
For the owner of the world has interlocked creation and
   death
Inseparably like mating dogs.

ESHU *breaks out into a jerking mocking dance and sings:*
When I walk through the groundnuts
Only the tuft of my hair is visible.
If I weren't such a huge fellow,
I would not be visible at all.
When I am angry I hit a stone until it bleeds,
When I am angry, I sit on the skin of an ant.
The stone I throw today
Has killed a bird of yesterday.

    ESHU *continues to dance, while a chorus of women is heard
    from behind the scene.*

WOMEN (*off*): Young ones never hear the death of cloth
– Cloth only wears to shreds.
– Old ones never hear the death of cloth
Cloth only wears to shreds.
Young ones never hear the death of Obatala
– Cloth only wears to shreds.
Old ones never hear the death of Obatala
– Cloth only wears to shreds.

CURTAIN

Everyman

CHARACTERS

OLODUMARE, *God*

IKU, *Death*

EVERYMAN

EVERYMAN'S COMPANION

SERVANT

COOK

POOR NEIGHBOUR

DEBTOR

DEBTOR'S WIFE

HARLOT

FAT COUSIN

THIN COUSIN

EVERYMAN'S DAUGHTER

BABATUNDE

FRIENDS, POLICEMEN, MUSICIANS

OWO, *Money*

GOOD DEEDS

On a raised platform, OLODUMARE *sits on his throne. He is dressed like an Oba, in agbada and beaded crown, but all in white. The white beads hanging from his crown cover his face entirely. At his side stand two small* SWORDBEARERS. *They wear loincloths and hold the ada, the ceremonial sword, that is the symbol of the power over life and death.*

The play opens with the chorus of SWORDBEARERS, *which is repeated at the end of the scene.*

SWORDBEARERS: Olodumare
  Owner of the world
  In the kingdom where the sun goes to rest
  You sit on your throne
  You hold us in your hand
  And we weigh lightly.
  You only decide
  Whether we may return
  To challenge fate once more
  On earth
  Or whether – our characters beyond repair –
  We'll be condemned to the heaven of potsherds
  Never to return
  Never to try again.
OLODUMARE: Truly I am tired of the children of the world.
  Their origin in heaven they forget —
  Living worse than beasts.
  I gave them eyes – they refuse to see.
  I gave them ears – they refuse to hear.

I gave them brains – they refuse to remember.
Look at Everyman enjoying his wealth.
He has children, he has houses, he has lorries:
And his money increases and has children;
And his money multiplies and has grandchildren.
But he forgets,
Money does not prevent a man from becoming a fool.
Money does not prevent a man from becoming mad.
The red feather is the pride of the parrot.
The young leaf is the pride of the palm-tree.
The sun is the pride of heaven:
But wisdom – not money – is the pride of man!
Everyman treats money like his God:
He sacrifices to him every day:
He sacrifices his wisdom, he sacrifices his friendship,
He sacrifices his compassion;
He sacrifices every virtue to money.
He has forgotten that day in heaven
When, fifty years ago, he knelt before my throne
To receive his fate.
Then Everyman prayed for money – and his request was
     granted,
For he said:
Money shall be my tool to do great works:
Money shall be my bricks and my cement;
Money shall be my spade and my hoe;
Money shall be my slave – to work
For the improvement of my town!
Now I am tired of Everyman,
For he broke his promise.
He uses money to destroy – not to build.
Instead of building his town – he rules it.
Instead of helping his people – he buys them.
Instead of sharing his wealth – he hoards it.

Therefore I have decided
A sudden judgement day I will hold
And deal with Everyman according to his merit.
Iku! Iku!

IKU: My Lord,
Owner of the sun, owner of the sky, owner of the world.
Nobody knows your father,
The liars are only lying;
Nobody knows your mother,
The liars are only lying.

OLODUMARE: Iku,
You the most faithful of all my servants!
Go you to Everyman with my urgent message:
He must set out on a pilgrimage at once
Today, this very hour, do I want to see him
Before my throne.
Without delay he must appear
And let him bring his book of accounts.

IKU: My Lord,
I shall run through the whole world
And I will visit all those who do not
Know your laws. I will find them, in every
Nook and corner of the world, those
Who have forgotten their promises
Made before they were born!
And I shall strike them suddenly
And hard: and their eyes will break
And their knees collapse, and their blood
Will curdle. And without delay,
They must set out on their pilgrimage.

IKU *goes out.*

The PROLOGUE *closes with a repeat of the* SWORD
BEARERS' *opening chorus.*

CURTAIN

In front of EVERYMAN'*s house.* EVERYMAN *enters with his*
COMPANION.

EVERYMAN: My friend I beg you: go back to the house
  And call my servant: I have forgotten
  Something important.
      COMPANION *hurries off.*
  It is true, I cannot complain:
  In all the town there is none
  More respected than I.
  My money multiplies daily,
  There is nobody in this town
  Whom I could not buy! When
  I enter the palace, the drummers
  Forget the praise names of the king
  And let the air resound with my name:
  Everyman, commander of money,
  Everyman. owner of the town,
  Everyman, owner of the world!
      COMPANION *returns with* SERVANT.
  Sule,
  Go into my room, and bring that packet of pound notes
  I forgot on my desk. And call me the cook,
  Important strangers are expected today
  And a feast must be prepared in haste.
      SERVANT *enters the house.* COOK *emerges at once.*
  I want you to cook for twenty guests today,
  And give us the best.

COOK: Excuse Sah!
  Make a de cook fresh one?
  Because *egusi* soup remain plenty for pot
  And so so goat meat of yesterday.
EVERYMAN: You big-eared fool! You flatfooted idiot!
  Am I a beggar, to feed on leftovers?
  Get into your kitchen and do as you are told!
      COOK *goes out.*
      The SERVANT *comes out of the house and hands over the
      money. The* POOR NEIGHBOUR *emerges from the back-
      ground, and approaches fearfully.*
EVERYMAN (*to his companion*): You my friend and companion
      of many years,
  Take this money, and hurry down to Bisi,
  My lady-lover. Tell her to come to my party
  And bring the best Highlife band
  She can find. And give her these few notes —
  For these independent women and
  Lip-painted ladies have many needs
  And great pride. Let her go and buy
  What she desires and let her heart
  Be happy when she comes. This money
  Will get her velvet cloth, rekyi rekyi,
  Sarasobia scent, fine pomade, gold and silver,
  Headtie, handkerchiefs, umbrella, shoes,
  Shirt and blouse, iron bed, blanket and
  Bed sheets, pillows and pillow-cases,
  Sleeping-gowns, easy chairs, door blinds,
  Window blinds, mosquito-net, table and
  Table-cloth, carpets, bed curtains,
  Handwatch, looking-glass, powder,
  Sewing-machine, portmanteaux, trunk box,
  Bicycle, gramophone and so many other
  Things a woman could use.

  C

POOR NEIGHBOUR (*prostrates himself*): Master, I beg you,
  help me
  I am in trouble.
COMPANION: Do you know this man?
EVERYMAN: Who are you? I don't remember
  Seeing you before.
POOR NEIGHBOUR: I am Adeleke, Sir, the son of Kunle.
  I have known better days than these, Sir.
  I was your neighbour, once,
  Lived in that pretty house right next door.
  But I ran into debt and was driven out!
EVERYMAN: All right, all right! (*He hands him a coin.*)
POOR NEIGHBOUR (*refusing to take it*): Threepence?
  That is a poor gift. If you would
  Share that wad of notes with me,
  My worries could be over.
EVERYMAN: Ah-ah? Is that all?
COMPANION: If you gave him that,
  You would have a thousand beggars
  After you tomorrow!
POOR NEIGHBOUR: This money, I know, is nothing to you.
  If you spend it ten times over,
  You only need to beckon your servant,
  And he'll bring you the same amount from your house.
EVERYMAN: You foolish man!
  Do you know what it means to be a rich man?
  Do you think it is easy?
  'A rich man!' That is easily said.
  But we rich people lead a hard life,
  If you knew it,
  You might not want to change with me.
  My money can never sit still:
  It must run here and there,
  Work for me and travel and fight.

Money must marry more money
And get pregnant with more money.
A rich man has no easy life:
His lorries break down
And want to be mended.
The price of cocoa falls
And petrol goes up.
One's children go to school
They study abroad, their dowry
Must be paid when they marry.
Do you think it is easy to maintain
All these houses and cars and farms
The children and wives and servants?
Do you think that money grows on a tree?
No work is harder than collecting debts and rents!
If I would listen to fellows like you,
I could not make three steps
Without opening my hand.
You think it is easy! But suppose
All my property was divided equally
Among all those who are in need —
Do you think your share would be bigger,
Than these threepence here?

> EVERYMAN *throws down the threepence. The* POOR
> NEIGHBOUR *picks it up and leaves.*

COMPANION: You answered him well,
You put him in his place!
Money makes a man wise,
I can see that indeed.
But now farewell – and let me hurry
To Bisi and invite her to the feast.

> *He goes out.*
> *The* DEBTOR *enters, led by two policemen; behind him the*
> DEBTOR'S WIFE *and* CHILDREN, *poorly dressed.*

EVERYMAN: Who is that chap, I wonder,
  With his arms tied on his back?
  I guess he failed to pay his debts
  Now he'll have time to think about his folly,
  Cutting grass with his fellow prisoners.
DEBTOR: There are many whose account book is not in order.
  They are enjoying their life,
  And forget that one day
  They will be called before the judge.
EVERYMAN: Whom do you mean by that?
DEBTOR: Always the one who asks.
EVERYMAN: What are you talking about?
  Who do you take me for?
DEBTOR: If I was in your place,
  I would feel ashamed.
EVERYMAN: If you are in trouble,
  Is it my fault?
DEBTOR: Was it not your lawyer who took me to court?
  Could you not give me another chance?
EVERYMAN: Who advised you to become a borrower?
  My money does not distinguish between people:
  It knows neither you nor me,
  But it must have its due!
  You have none to blame but yourself!
DEBTOR: See the rich man,
  Mocking a man in his need.
  How easy it would be for him
  To save my children from starvation.
  But he is hard as stone.
DEBTOR'S WIFE: Have you no pity at all on my children?
  Could you not tear the cursed debtor's note?
  With all your wealth, you would not feel the loss.
  Can you stand there and watch,
  Now my children are driven to beg in the streets?

EVERYMAN: You talk of things you do not understand.
　　Money is like everything else in the world,
　　There are rules and laws to govern its movements.
DEBTOR: Oh money, money is a treacherous and evil crea-
　　　　ture,
　　If you stretch out your hand for it, it swallows you.
　　If we desire it, we fall into its power.
　　Now I must suffer for my miserable greed.
EVERYMAN: You are quick to curse like a fool!
　　Why do you pretend to despise money?
　　Money was your orisha, money was your oracle,
　　Money was your father, money was your mother.
　　Why do you try to renounce it now?
　　Blessed is the day when money was invented!
　　Money has power over any other thing:
　　There is no house, no land, no wife it cannot buy.
　　Money is more powerful than armies,
　　It is more powerful than judges and kings.
　　Money is the most faithful servant
　　To the man who owns it.
　　There is nothing it refuses to do.
　　There is nothing it cannot do.
　　It is the money I hold in my hand
　　That raises me high above you.
　　Had you known how to deal with money
　　You would not be on your way to prison now!
　　　　The policemen carry the DEBTOR *off to prison. His* WIFE
　　　　and CHILDREN *follow, weeping.*
EVERYMAN: I do not know why I waste my time
　　With people like him,
　　Who make me ill-tempered.
　　I should be happy now and get into the mood
　　To receive my guests and make them feel
　　That they have come to the house of Everyman,

Everyman the money commander,
Everyman owner of the town, owner of the world!
But something oppresses me today.
The very thought of music makes me sad.
The thought of drink even makes me sick.
Yet I am not ill —
Something spoils my pleasure today:
Something worries my head —
Something like fear.
But why should I feel fear?
No man was more secure than I.
Nobody dares to raise his hand against me:
I buy and sell them all.
No beautiful women will refuse my love —
I buy and sell them all. Yet I am sad today?

> *A* BABALAWO *– oracle priest – is passing. He is an old man,
> poorly dressed. He takes no notice of* EVERYMAN *and slowly
> walks past. When* EVERYMAN *sees him he calls out.*

EVERYMAN: You father of secrets!
Who lives on the foolishness of others.
You who thrive on the credulity
Of old women and children.
If you say you know secrets —
Can you tell me the secret of my sadness?

BABALAWO: Everyman,
Who calls himself commander of money:
To insult me is a small matter,
For I am only old man.
But no one has yet insulted Orunmila
The God of fate – and has gone unpunished.

EVERYMAN: Little I care for your oracle and god:
Look at me! Did you throw the nuts for me
Before I became rich?
Did I consult you, before I gained power?

If you can see the future —
Why are you so poor?
And if you know secrets —
Why can't you explain to me,
Why I am so sad?

BABALAWO: No Babalawo likes to work for the likes of you.
But if you wish to consult the oracle
I have no right to refuse.

EVERYMAN: Well let it be then,
Throw your nuts.

He throws him a small coin.

Let me hear your lies,
It will pass the time,
While I wait for my guests.

The BABALAWO *kneels down and spreads out his utensils on the floor. He throws his palmnuts and draws his signs in the sand. Then he recites the Odu.*

BABALAWO: Ogbe went hunting in the bush.
He was told to sacrifice,
Lest he should meet disaster there.
But he refused to sacrifice.
When he went into the bush
Rain started to beat him hard.
Ogbe took shelter in a big hole.
Was it an ant hole? Was it a tree hole?
No! it was the anus of an elephant.
The elephant closed his anus —
Ogbe prayed – but could not escape.
His relatives searched for him in the bush
They brought the sacrifice:
The same sacrifice, that he had refused.
Then the elephant passed him out with his shit.

EVERYMAN: You impudent old rascal! You father of lies!
Are you trying to frighten me

With the fear of death?
Do you think you can fool me,
Because you want to get fat
On the sacrifice you ask me to bring?
> *Highlife music is heard approaching from a distance.*
Get out! My guests are coming.
Let them not find you here, to spoil their fun.

BABALAWO: I am going:
But Everyman!
Listen to my final warning:
When the banana dies – its children succeed it.
But when the fire dies – it covers its face with ashes.
> *As the* BABALAWO *goes out, a gay crowd of guests is streaming in, led by the* HARLOT, *who is gaudily dressed.*

EVERYMAN: Welcome, welcome my friend! Wole kososi!
Come in, and make yourselves at home!
Sule! Sule!
> *The* SERVANT *enters.*
Bring drinks and food.
Serve my guests and make everyone happy.
> *The guests sit down. The servants pass round food and drink.*
> *The band installs itself to the left and plays soft highlife music.*
> *The conversation of the guests can be heard on top of the music.*
> EVERYMAN *is seated in the centre, the* HARLOT *by his side.*

HARLOT (*kneels beside* EVERYMAN): Eku nawo O! Eku nawo
O!
Everyman, thank you for your gift.

EVERYMAN: Nothing is too good for you, Bisi!
You are the blackest girl in town,
Your neck is longer, your hips are rounder
Than any other girl's.
You make me forget my fifty years,
You make me feel young and gay like a boy.

HARLOT: Oh do not talk about your age.

I have no interest in young boys
And their corner corner love.
They want to go to bed with you
And can't even afford to buy you a pair of shoes!
EVERYMAN: If a man was reminded of his death,
   And he was overcome by sadness and fear,
   Merely to look at you my dear
   Would make him feel glad again.
HARLOT: I do not like the way you talk tonight.
   You think too much. You make me afraid.
   Let the band play to discard your worries!
      The band strikes up a noisy highlife tune. They all join in
      the song.
ALL: Everyman owns the world,
   Everyman has children
   Everyman has servants
   Everyman has wives
   Everyman has houses.
   Everyman treats money like his slave!
   He sends him to bring food,
   He sends him to bring drink,
   He sends him to bring woman,
   And the slave obeys!
EVERYMAN: Thank you, thank you my friends all,
   For coming to lead me to my grave.
CONFUSED VOICES: What?
   Did he say grave?
   Is the man sick?
EVERYMAN: I am sorry, I don't know what my tongue is
      saying:
   I mean to say:
   Thank you for coming to enjoy with me today.
   And welcome to my house.
HARLOT: Pay no attention my friends.

My master feels feverish tonight,
But he will soon be better.
Eat and drink and be merry!
> *The* HARLOT *sits down beside* EVERYMAN *and looks at him, worried.*

HARLOT: Everyman, are you ill?
You sit there and stare,
Like a man shaken by fever.

EVERYMAN: Bisi, I fear, I fear:
As I am looking at them there
My guests look cold and fleshless;
Their skulls are bald, they stare at me
From empty sockets, like the dead risen from their graves!

HARLOT: You are ill, my lord, your mind is confused,
Let me lead you into the house.

EVERYMAN: Ha, ha! What a crazy thought!
What silly visions and dreams.
Bring me some beer that will clear the brain.

FAT COUSIN: Everyman, you look sad today.
Have you got worries?
Surely there's nothing that can worry you?
All problems will be solved,
By money your faithful slave!

EVERYMAN: Yes . . . yes . . . it is so . . .
Only, you know,
As I was looking at you all
Sitting down there and drinking
I suddenly thought
That I could buy you all and sell you again,
And it wouldn't trouble me more
Than the bite of a fly.

THIN COUSIN: What is the meaning of this rude speech?

FAT COUSIN: He is not used to talk like that!

A GUEST: This is a rich man's talk:

Conceited and impudent!

HARLOT: Was your speech also meant for me?

    EVERYMAN *stares at her.*

What is the matter? What have I done?

Why are you looking at me like that?

EVERYMAN: I do not know, what has come over me my love,

But I was thinking just now:

And I wondered: what would you look like

If you heard the news, that I must die this hour?

HARLOT: What foolish thoughts are these?

Wake up from these dreams,

I am here at your side

And yours for ever.

EVERYMAN: And if I asked you to follow me to heaven?

Would you have courage to follow me?

Oh no, I'd rather not ask you.

It would increase my suffering,

To see your blood go cold, your knees weak;

To see you break out in sweat

And make excuses and break your vow!

I dare not think of the time,

When you withdraw from my embrace

And let me face my last hour alone. (*He sighs.*)

HARLOT: My friends,

I am worried about Everyman.

He is not happy and relaxed,

As we have known him.

His speech is confused and his head

Is disturbed by fever.

My friends,

What can we do?

FAT COUSIN: It is the good life and excess of drink,

That is now troubling his heart.

THIN COUSIN: He should be cured with herbs

And sacred leaves. I do not believe
In the white man's foreign medicine
When it comes to troubles of the mind.
I can take him to a Babalawo
Whose knowledge surpasses all hospitals.

A GUEST: For God's sake let's have music.
A good tune has cured many a sickness!

ANOTHER GUEST: Yes, music! Let's have music!

EVERYMAN: I am sorry, my friends;
I have been sad tonight
And a bad host.
How could the guests be merry,
When the host is sick, his brain
Confused with fever?
Forgive me.
But I am better now: this beer,
This cool refreshing drink
Has cleared my brain.
So let us have music and enjoy ourselves.

   The band plays 'Nylon dress, is a fine fine dress', *and all join in the song. Distant drumming is heard off stage.* EVERYMAN *pushes his glass away.*

EVERYMAN: This drumming is strange,
What can it mean?
The State drums sound
As in times of war,
A deathly and fearful sound.

FAT COUSIN: I did not hear a thing.

THIN COUSIN: Has anybody heard drumming?

A GUEST: Are you talking of drumming?

HARLOT: I beg you my friends,
Continue with your song.

   The band takes up 'Nylon dress' *again.*

VOICES (*off stage*): Everyman! Everyman! Everyman!

EVERYMAN *jumps up in fear.*

EVERYMAN: My God, who is calling me
With this terrible voice?
My friends, my friends,
Who is calling so?

COMPANION: Everyman, I am here at your side.
What is your trouble, what can I do?

EVERYMAN: My friends, my friends,
Who has been calling 'Everyman'
In this terrible voice?

THIN COUSIN: It must have been the echo of our song
That you mistook for calling.

EVERYMAN: No, no, a terrible sound,
More fearful than the oro at night,
More frightening than witches' cries
A roaring, screaming sound,
Strange and yet terribly familiar
It called my name . . .
There there again, I here them calling
'Everyman!'

VOICES (*off stage*): Everyman! Everyman! Everyman!

HARLOT: I do not hear a thing.

FAT COUSIN: Not a sound.

COMPANION: An illusion, my friend, you look unwell.
Shall I not lead you into the house?

EVERYMAN: As you are talking to me so
My strength comes back into my limbs.
The terrible sound is fading in my ears.
I promise you,
Tomorrow shall I go to the Babalawo,
To cure this trouble in my brain.
Continue with the feast my friends!

They all continue to eat and drink noisily. EVERYMAN
suddenly jumps up fearfully.

EVERYMAN: Help, help, my friends,
   I can hear it approach.
   Steps approaching, getting louder
   Coming upon me from behind.
   No earthly being walks like that!
      IKU *suddenly appears at some distance. All the guests rise.*
IKU: Everyman! Can you enjoy yourself,
   With music and drink and harlots,
   And forget your creator?
EVERYMAN: What question is this
   Put at such hour?
   What business of yours?
   Who are you anyhow?
IKU: Olodumare has sent me to you
   In haste.
   That's why I am here.
EVERYMAN: Olodumare, sent for me?
      He grips his heart.
   Oh, it is so, it is so.
IKU: I have come to fetch you,
   Get ready now.
   To give account of your life
   Before the throne of Olodumare
EVERYMAN: To give account?
   I am not ready yet!
   And who are you?
   I do not know you, messenger.
IKU: I am Iku, I fear no man.
   I spare nobody. When I am sent,
   I strike without mercy!
      Screaming among the guests. Many make their escape.
EVERYMAN: I am not ready yet.
   You come unannounced
   And want to seize me at the height of life.

My account book is not yet prepared
If you could give me ten, twelve years,
I would bring everything in order,
And come, prepared, on my pilgrimage
To meet Olodumare before his throne.

IKU: Your prayers are in vain.
Your presence is required now.

EVERYMAN: Olodumare, on your throne in Heaven,
Have mercy on me in my need.
Shall I alone go in this trip,
Shall none of my friends be at my side,
When all my life
I could not bear to be without company?

IKU: Company and parties have come to an end.
From now on, you are alone.
Or did you think that all your property
Would follow you on your trip?
Did you not know that these possessions
Never were your own, but only lent to you?

EVERYMAN: Give me one day!
Give me this night at least,
Until the break of day!

IKU: Such requests cannot be put to me.
When I approach a man,
I strike him quick.
I strike his heart without delay
And he must follow me without warning.

EVERYMAN (*prostrating himself*): Give me small time, I beg,
To ask my friends,
Which one of them will accompany me
And help me when I face my judge.

IKU: No one will follow you —
Rest you assured.

EVERYMAN: Only one hour!

IKU: So let it be.
  But use your time,
  For in one hour sharp
  You have to follow me
  And no more pleading
  Can help you then.

  IKU *goes out.*

EVERYMAN: My good companion, you know . . .

COMPANION: I know.
  I saw how death approached you suddenly,
  A man in his best years and health.
  My heart was beating in my throat
  With fear and pity.
  Oh Everyman, I was your friend in all these years,
  I shall not leave you at this hour.
  So tell me now, what you still need
  And I can do.

EVERYMAN: My friend!

COMPANION: Speak freely! Do not hesitate to ask.
  Whatever you say, it will be done.
  I am your servant to the last.

  EVERYMAN *wants to speak.*

  Say, if anyone has harmed you in your life,
  And gone unpunished let me know.
  This hand shall bring you vengeance
  And you shall be satisfied.

EVERYMAN: Oh no, not that my friend, not that.

COMPANION: Your properties are worrying you then.
  And who shall be the benefactor of your will.
  Let me but know your wish – and rest assured
  It will be done just as you say.

EVERYMAN: No, no my friend, it is not that.

COMPANION: I know it's Bisi, not your wives
  You wish your riches to enjoy.

EVERYMAN: My friend, please listen . . .

COMPANION: No need to talk, I've understood!

EVERYMAN: My friend, companion of my youth,
My problem is a different one.
I have been ordered to proceed
To heaven; to give account of all my life.
The road is long and tiresome and I fear
To face the judgement by myself.
I need a friend to follow me, to plead for me
Before Olodumare. I'm ill prepared, I need
Your help. Unless you beg for me
Before the throne of the owner of heaven
I'll be condemned to go to the heaven of potsherds,
And never again be given a chance,
To try my luck and fortune on this earth.

COMPANION: My friend, whatever you may ask of me
To do for you on this earth – I will perform.
But to follow you when you are called by Iku – never!
I fear the road, the darkness and the river
We have to cross, I am myself not yet prepared
To meet Olodumare.
Farewell my friend, I wish you luck,
But give me leave to go, my wife and child
Wait me at home.

EVERYMAN: Wait! Wait! A minute more!

COMPANION (*hurrying away*): Farewell, good luck to you!

EVERYMAN: No one had better friends than I:
They called me money commander and owner of the
world.
Whenever I had a feast like tonight,
They came to sing my praises: owner of the town
They called me and enjoyed themselves.
Alas! where are they now?
He notices the two cousins who are still sitting drinking.

My cousins Ho! Are you still here?
I knew that you would stick by me.
My friends have left. But blood they say,
Is thicker than water. I knew you would
Not leave your own dear relative
To his cold fate.

FAT COUSIN: Everyman: is there anything you wish?
Anything we can do, before you set out
On your last journey?

THIN COUSIN: Speak up, and let us know. Be quick.
Any minute now Iku may return
And take you away.

EVERYMAN: My cousins, my own blood:
Stand you by me in the hour of need.

FAT COUSIN: We told you, Everyman, we are yours
And shall never desert you.

THIN COUSIN: Your last wish on this world
It shall be fulfilled!
Truly I promise you.

EVERYMAN: My cousins both: have mercy on me.
For I am unprepared to give account
Of all my days before the throne of heaven.
My account book is ill-kept, huge debts
I have not paid; and my good deeds
I have almost forgotten.
Therefore accompany me, cousins dear,
Be at my side. Help me on the long
And tiresome road. Hold you my hands
When I must cross the dark and fearsome river
Prostrate you to Olodumare and beg for me —
For I am ill prepared.

FAT COUSIN: To follow you there?

THIN COUSIN: Not on my life!

FAT COUSIN: Leave my belongings?

THIN COUSIN: Leave my wife?

FAT COUSIN: I cannot go one step!

THIN COUSIN: I fear the road!

FAT COUSIN: I'm ill-prepared myself!

THIN COUSIN: My own account is never made.

FAT COUSIN: Farewell!

THIN COUSIN: Good luck!

FAT COUSIN: Iku is coming – we must leave.

They rush out.

EVERYMAN: Only an hour ago – I still had power
Over them all.
I commanded them – and they obeyed.
I bought them and I sold them as I pleased.
Has Iku so quickly stripped me of my power?
Am I already naked and deserted,
Even before my journey has begun?
Ha!
But Owo my most faithful servant
Shall not leave me now.
My friends and cousins have deserted me
But Owo shall be at my side.
Sule! Sule!!

SERVANT: Yes master, I am here.

EVERYMAN: Go to the house and bring my money box.
Bring me that great big heavy box
That's in my bedroom.
Bring it at once!

SULE *disappears and returns with several other servants
carrying a large, heavy box. They place it centre stage.*

You may leave!

The servants retire.

I am afraid, Iku is near.
Sweat pours down my neck,
My belly is like water.

I cannot recognize myself.
Who am I? Am I not Everyman?
The rich man? The popular man?
Is this not my hand? Is this not my gown?
Is that not my money? My treasure?
Ah, Owo, do not desert me!

He kneels down beside the box and prostrates to it.

Stand you by me, my faithful servant.
If you remain with me
I'll fear no journey and no judgement,
I'll bother not about Iku!

The lid of the box is thrown open, and OWO, *personified,
jumps out.* OWO *is beautifully dressed in very rich cloth and
holds a grinning mask in front of his face.*

OWO: Everyman, what's wrong with you?
I see you getting hot and cold,
Your dress is wet with sweat
And butterflies are fluttering in your stomach.

EVERYMAN: But who are you?

OWO: So you don't know me by face?
I am Owo your servant
I am Owo your only friend in this world.

EVERYMAN: Owo, my friend,
The sight of you gladdens my heart.
No friend more loyal, no servant more faithful
Did I have in this world.
What I desired you bought —
What I hated you destroyed.
At my command, you would put any woman
Into my bed and any man into jail.
Your commander I was all these years,
Now listen, for I shall command you
For the last time.

OWO: Say what you need – I'll shun no work

And no pain to supply your wants.

EVERYMAN: My problem is another one —

I had a message . . .

OWO: A message? And from whom?

EVERYMAN (*lowers his eyes, and speaks softly*): Yes, the
  messenger has come . . .

OWO: So sudden? Well, it's a surprise!

EVERYMAN: It's true – but you will follow me!

OWO: Follow you? That cannot be.

EVERYMAN: You are my property – do as you are told!

OWO: Your property? Ah, what a joke!

EVERYMAN: Will you revolt?

I'll show you back into your place!

You, slave!

> OWO *throws away the grinning mask. A fearful face* (*drawn
> in heavy make-up*) *appears underneath. He pushes* EVERY-
> MAN *aside.*

OWO: I'll teach you who I am!

You dwarf!

How dare you think I am your slave?

EVERYMAN: Did I not command you at every hour?

OWO: Did I not rule in your heart and your soul?

EVERYMAN: Did you not serve me in the house and in the
  town?

OWO: Did I not fool you all your life?

How big, you felt yourself —

Owner of properties, owner of men.

You bought and sold, you commanded and ruled.

Like a peacock you strutted around,

Who displays his feathers to his hens.

Now you are naked and alone

Like a newly born swallow fallen from its nest.

Where are your friends, your harlots, now?

Was I your slave?

Well now: you'll make your trip,
Alone, a small and naked fool.
I'll stay right here – to play with other men.
   He pushes EVERYMAN *down – and leaves.* GOOD DEEDS,
   a very sick old woman, stumbles on to the stage and collapses,
   exhausted.
GOOD DEEDS (*feebly*): Everyman . . .
   Everyman, can't you hear?
EVERYMAN: A sick old woman there – I have no time for her.
GOOD DEEDS: Everyman!
EVERYMAN: Leave me alone – I have got worries of my own.
GOOD DEEDS: I do belong to you —
   For your sake, I lie here.
EVERYMAN: What do you mean?
GOOD DEEDS: I'm your good works, I came to follow you
   On your long trip.
   Before the throne of Heaven
   I came to witness on your behalf.
   Alas, I am too weak.
   Throughout your life, you have neglected me,
   Now I am old and sick
   And I can go no farther.
EVERYMAN: Oh what a fool I was – you my true friend
   I have neglected all my life.
   I loved Owo too much, the false friend
   Who has now deserted me. He fooled my senses
   Made me blind with drink, proud with possessions
   Vain with women, drunk with power.
   Oh he made me waste my life.
   Empty handed and friendless now,
   Must I confront Olorun?
   Woe unto me:
   My promises were broken – my life was wasted
   And to the potsherd heaven shall I be condemned.

*IKU enters from the right side. He waits a while. During the
following he comes very slowly nearer. At the same time,
SIDIKATU, EVERYMAN's daughter, appears from the left
and approaches her father slowly. She is highly pregnant.*

EVERYMAN: Sidikatu, my daughter!
  Are you the only one of all my friends and relatives
  Who even comes to say good-bye to me?
  Look at your father:
  Who was commander of money
  Owner of the world.
  You grew up in the false glory of my power.
  You saw me handling people like property.
  Look at me now: no child will obey my commands.
  Look at my life wasted, my good works
  Exhausted and neglected, dying at my side.
  I am afraid, Sidikatu,
  I feel Iku is on his way
    IKU approaches from the back.
  I feel a chill going down my back
  My daughter, wipe the sweat from my brow,
  Leave me not now: hold my hand, pray for me.
SIDIKATU: My father:
  How can I speak; what can I say,
  When I see you like this.
  I grew up in the shadow of your power.
  You cared little for me, had little time for me;
  But I admired your might.
  You fulfilled my wishes, I felt secure,
  Thought you were second to God.
  Oh how was I deceived:
  To see you miserable now, and small and shaking.
EVERYMAN: Curse me not, my daughter.
  I feel he is coming —
  Now.

IKU *stands directly behind him.*
Help me, oh comfort me, my child.
SIDIKATU: My father,
Be not despaired.
The owner of heaven may forgive you.
You have betrayed his trust
You have broken your promises —
But let us pray for another chance.
Let us pray, that you may return,
Come back to earth to start your life once more.
Let us pray for another beginning.
EVERYMAN (*wildly*): Oh let me try again!
Olodumare, owner of heaven,
Owner of the sun!
Grant me another beginning,
That I may prove myself.
IKU *raises his hand above him.*
Iku, I am ready now . . .
Let me but end this prayer!
Olodumare, owner of heaven
Owner of the sun!
Bless the fruit which my daughter
Carries in her belly.
Forgive my breach of promise —
And through her,
Grant me another beginning.
Let me . . .
At this moment IKU *strikes.* EVERYMAN *screams and falls*
dead. SIDIKATU *breaks out into wailing.*

CURTAIN

SIDIKATU *is seen with a baby in her arms. She is consulting a* BABALAWO. *As the curtain rises the* BABALAWO *is throwing his nuts and drawing his lines on the board. Finally he recites the Odu.*

BABALAWO: The father was asked to sacrifice
But he did not sacrifice.
So when the son planted
The birds came to scatter the fruit
And the rats came to eat the roots.
And poverty shall sit on his head
And debt will hang round his neck,
And nakedness will expose his bottom.
This child shall go through life in poverty:
But remember:
Money does not prevent a man from being blind;
Money does not prevent a man from being lame;
Money does not prevent a man from being mad;
Money does not prevent a man from being a fool.
Therefore let him come and think again
And let him select wisdom and sacrifice.
The sacrifice is a fish, a mouse, two hundred bean cakes,
And five shillings.
Red feathers are the pride of the parrot,
Young leaves are the pride of the palm-tree,
White flowers are the pride of cotton,
A straight tree is the pride of the forest,
A fast antelope is the pride of the bush;

A beautiful woman is the pride of the husband,
The rainbow is the pride of heaven,
Children are the pride of the mother
The moon and stars are the pride of the sun
And wisdom is the pride of man!

SIDIKATU: Father of secrets:
Your nuts portend poverty and suffering
For my child. But I will do as you say:
I will sacrifice and pray, that the child
Though poor, shall be wise; that the child
Though hungry shall be good; that the child
Though penniless shall be loved.
Father of secrets!
Now throw your nuts again and ask:
How shall we call this child,
And whether perhaps one of his forefathers . . .
Maybe . . .
Oh ask: how shall we call this child?

BABALAWO (*throws his nuts again, then speaks*): There is no
pregnant woman,
Who cannot give birth to a father of secrets,
There is no woman
Who cannot give birth to Orunmila himself.
If a father has begotten a child —
However long it may take,
The child may yet beget the father.
If a mother gave birth to a child
She may still be born by that child.
For Orunmila said:
I shall bring heaven to earth
And earth to heaven:
So your child shall be called BABATUNDE.

SIDIKATU: Orunmila, owner of heaven, be praised!
Praised be the owner of the sun

For granting us a new beginning!
Olodumare,
Nobody knows your father,
The liars are only lying!
Nobody knows your mother,
The liars are only lying.
You gave us a new beginning!
You will see another life:
For Owo shall be banished from this child's life:
Greed and avarice and lust for power
Shall be driven from his doorstep!
For he has come back to think again
And to choose anew:
If poverty sits on his head – he will not care.
If hunger hangs round his neck – he will not mind.
If nakedness uncovers his bottom – he will not be ashamed.
For he has come to choose wisdom – the pride of man.
    She jumps up and dances.
Babatunde O! Babatunde O! Babatunde O!
    At this point the whole cast rush on to the stage and surround
    her. They dance around her shouting Babatunde O! *Finally*
    they range themselves on the front of the stage and in a final
    dance EVERYMAN *leads the Chorus.*
CHORUS: There is no pregnant woman
Who cannot give birth to a father of secrets.
There is no father who has born a child
Who cannot be reborn by the child.
There is no mother
Who could not be reborn by her daughter.
Babatunde O!
A new beginning has been granted.
Let the child remember
That the red feathers are the pride of the parrot;
The horns are the pride of the bull;

The stars are the pride of the sun;
The spots are the pride of the leopard;
That loyalty is the pride of the dog —
But wisdom is the pride of man.

CURTAIN

Woyengi

Based on an Ijaw myth recorded by Gabriel Okara

CHARACTERS

WOYENGI, *the great mother; goddess of creation*

OGBOINBA, *a childless woman, in possession of magic powers*

LAKPE, *her friend, mother of many children*

ISEMBI, *the king of the forest*

OLOKUN, *the king of the sea*

COCK, *ruler of 'the last kingdom of things that die'*

CREATURES *of Woyengi*

SWORDBEARERS

SPIRIT POWERS

SCENE I

Heaven. The stage is bare, except for a platform and a huge sun,
suspended high. WOYENGI, *the great mother, is seated on a*
raised platform surrounded by SWORDBEARERS. *Before her*
crouches a figure completely muffled in a brown cloth – symbol-
izing a lump of clay about to be moulded into human form by the
creator goddess. To WOYENGI'S *right stand about a dozen*
figures clad in white togas. They are newly created human beings,
who are waiting to choose their sex, destiny, and death from
WOYENGI *before going into the world.*

SWORDBEARERS: Woyengi,
  Mother of the world,
  You are bright and radiant like the sun
  When it rises in the east.
  Your feet walk the earth
  While your head towers in the sky.
  You command the sun and the moon
  You created the earth
  When you were lonely.
  You made thousands of creatures
  From your single form.
  You create the child
  In the mother's womb.
  You make the seed flow in man
  And the blood in woman.
  You nurse the child in the womb
  You give it breath
  You open its mouth

On the day of its birth
And let it speak.
You created the Niger
That flows to the sea in multiple streams
You placed the other Niger in the sky
That it may fall down and water the land.
Woyengi,
Mother of the world,
Your feet walk the earth
While your head towers in the sky.

> WOYENGI *now rises to the act of creation. She approaches the crouching figure which slowly rises following* WOYENGI's *movements.* WOYENGI *pulls out a naked arm from the cloth, then another, etc., until finally the cloth falls and the new creature appears, almost naked. The* SWORDBEARERS *lead the creature away to the right and clothe it in white. The mime of creation should be accompanied by very quiet, intimate music – if possible a xylophone. This should be in sharp contrast to the brisk fanfare of the praise song that precedes it.*

WOYENGI: My creatures, approach.
The world is waiting for you
With forests, rivers, towns and villages.
The heat of the sun you will feel
And the coolness of rain.
The land is there for you to work,
The forest to hunt in.
You will know the pain of birth,
The terror of death, and the happiness of love.
Come now and choose your fate.
But choose wisely:
Nobody can eat the words
He will speak here and now.
Once you have entered the world,
Screaming, through your mother's womb,

Your words will have lost the power of creation.
But for this brief moment between creation and birth
You share with me the power of the word.
Every wish you utter
Before you wade into the world
Through the river of life
Must come to pass.
Approach, then, my creatures,
And choose your fate.
Choose – but choose wisely:
Whether man or woman you wish to be,
What manner of life you wish to lead,
What to achieve on earth, how long to live —
And finally – most difficult choice of all —
You must select your death.

> *The* FIRST CREATURE *approaches boldly, kneels before the throne of* WOYENGI *and speaks. All subsequent* CREATURES *utter their wishes kneeling before* WOYENGI.

FIRST CREATURE: Woyengi,
Mother of the world,
You are bright and radiant like the sun
When it rises in the east.
Receive my words,
And bless my choice:
Let me be born a man, a real man,
A warrior. Let me live by the power of my arm,
Let me conquer and win,
Let me win fame and praise.
Do not prolong my life into feeble old age,
But in the prime of life
Let me die by the sword, by which I lived.
WOYENGI: So be it.
Arise, and take your life.

> *The* FIRST CREATURE *rises and moves over to the left. While*

D

the SECOND CREATURE *kneels before* WOYENGI, *he is being equipped by the* SWORDBEARERS *as a soldier. All the* CREATURES *are thus dressed and equipped before leaving for the world.*

SECOND CREATURE: Woyengi,
  You created the Niger,
  That flows into the sea in multiple rivers
  And you placed the other Niger in the sky
  That it may fall down and water the land.
  Mother of the world:
  Receive my words and bless my choice.
  Let me be born a man,
  A man rooted to the soil.
  Let me see the yam shoot climb up the pole
  Let me see corn gleam on the cob like teeth.
  Let me own the palm oil that oozes, redder than blood
  From the black kernel.
  Let me own the palm wine that hums,
  Milky white, in the calabash.
  Let me grow old, to see my children work the land
  Let me have grandchildren to bury me
  When I die quietly in my sleep:
WOYENGI: So be it:
  Arise and take your life.
THIRD CREATURE: Woyengi,
  Mother of the world.
  You created the sun that burns the land,
  That sits on man's brain
  And confuses him with fever.
  Woyengi,
  Mother of the world,
  You created the storm
  That floods the houses,
  Crushes the trees

And carries away the helpless fisherman,
And his canoe in black whirlpools.
Woyengi,
I fear the world and what it has in store for me:
Let me but peep at it.
Let me be a girl, to grow in the protection of the home:
But end my suffering soon:
In my seventh year let me return to you.
Let the sun, that is bright and radiant like yourself
Come and sit on my brain.
Let it carry me away in a mantle of fire,
Let it redeem me with its heat,
And return me to you.

WOYENGI: So be it.
What you have chosen must come to pass.
Arise and take your life.

FOURTH CREATURE: Woyengi,
Mother of the world.
You create the son in the mother's womb.
You make the seed flow in man,
You make the blood flow in woman.
You nurse the child in the womb,
You give it breath,
You open its mouth
On the day of its birth
And let it speak.
Woyengi,
Mother of the world —
Let me be a mother.
Let me be fruitful, and bear children
One, two, six, eight —
Let me bear children until my womb dries up.
Let me feel their toothless gums biting my breast,
Let me teach them to walk and to speak,

Let me live to see them bear children
In their turn.
Let me die suddenly
And with joy in my heart.
Woyengi,
Mother of the world —
Let me have children;
Give them breath,
Open their mouths on the day of birth
And let them speak.

WOYENGI: So be it.
Arise and take your life.

FIFTH CREATURE: Woyengi,
You who command the sun and the moon.
You who make the sap flow in the leaves,
You who gave poison to the puff-adder,
And healing power to the ginger-lily,
Let me have power!
Let me share your secrets.
Let me be a woman – but let my womb be dry.
Little I care for children or wealth.
Let me learn the secrets of herbs and leaves;
Teach me the language of the coockal and the hornbill.
Let me have power to heal and to kill.
Give me command over the word,
Let me mould the lives of men in my hand.
Woyengi,
You who gave poison to the puff-adder
And healing power to the ginger-lily,
Let me command the spirit,
Let me be second only to you —
And let me die,
When my heart bursts with power.

WOYENGI: Bold is your wish:

Unheard of your desire.
Yet so be it.
Arise and take your life.
But when you wade into the world
You shall not follow your fellow creatures
Through the muddy river of happiness and wealth.
You alone shall walk through the clear waters
Of the spirit. Your road shall be lonely and cold —
But your wish shall be fulfilled.

SWORDBEARERS: Woyengi,
Mother of the world.
The world lies in your hand,
As you have made it,
When you were lonely.
You made thousands of creatures
From your single being.
You give them breath,
You open their mouths
And let them speak.
Woyengi,
Mother of the world:
You alone make the sun rise in the east
Make the seed swell in the womb,
Woyengi, bright and radiant like the sun.

CURTAIN

SCENE II

The homes of LAKPE *and* OGBOINBA. *They are seen in their respective homes simultaneously. Their houses are indicated in the simplest possible fashion: three walls, open to the front. Where the stage is small, the two 'houses' could have a common wall in the middle, linked by a door.*

When the scene opens, LAKPE *is seen playing with her children, while* OGBOINBA *is attending to a patient.*

LAKPE (*sings, while she nurses the smallest child*): Why should you weep, Olukorondo?
A thorn never pricks a child's foot;
Don't I carry you on my back?
Why should you weep, Olukorondo?

    In the meantime the patient has left Ọ̀GBOINBA *and a group of people carry in an old woman, who seems to be in a bad state. Shouting and wailing goes on in* OGBOINBA'*s house, while* OGBOINBA *herself rushes about looking for medicine in her pots and calabashes. In the meantime* LAKPE'*s children have settled down to a catch game and can be heard over the din.*

ELDEST CHILD: Who has blood?
CHILDREN: Blood, blood.
ELDEST CHILD: Has a goat blood?
CHILDREN: Blood, blood.
ELDEST CHILD: Has a sheep blood?
CHILDREN: Blood, blood.
ELDEST CHILD: Has a dog blood?
CHILDREN: Blood, blood.

ELDEST CHILD: Has a stone blood?

YOUNGEST CHILD: Blood, blood!

Shrieks of laughter. The YOUNGEST CHILD *is being play-fully beaten. While the game was going on the old woman has received medicine and feels obviously better. Now* OGBOINBA *speaks comforting words to her.*

OGBOINBA: The tree that falls in the farm,
Does not kill people in the house.
The ceiling that crushes the bedroom,
Does not kill people in the street.
If the ulcer does not kill the person who has it,
The one who is washing it will not be ill.
The man lying down cannot fall.
The tree lying down casts no shadow.
Death claims many victims this year —
But since we were not borne together,
Why should we die together?

The woman is now able to walk with only slight support. After effusive thanks and greetings she is being led away. Now LAKPE *is heard singing to her child again, but during her song a hysterical patient is dragged into* OGBOINBA. *Four men try to hold him down, while he hits out in every direction and foams in the mouth.* OGBOINBA *calms him down at once with expert handling and gives him medicine to drink that puts him to sleep.*

LAKPE: A child is a rare bird,
A child is precious like coral.
You cannot buy a child on the market,
Not with all the money in the world.
The child you can buy is a slave —
But even if you have twenty slaves
And thirty servants —
Only a child brings you joy.
The buttocks of our child are not so flat

That we would tie the beads round another child's hips
One's child is one's child:
It may have a watery head, or a square head,
One's child is one's child:
Only one's child can bring one joy.

    OGBOINBA *has placed the patient on a couch. As the men who had brought him retreat with effusive thanks and greetings,* OGBOINBA *ties her headtie and leaves the house. She walks over to her friend* LAKPE. *She arrives in the middle of another game and she stands and watches, unobserved by the* CHILDREN *until the game is finished.*

ELDEST CHILD: Three birds came to the world
CHILDREN: From Olongo.
ELDEST CHILD: One was black as indigo
CHILDREN: From Olongo.
ELDEST CHILD: One was red as camwood
CHILDREN: From Olongo.
ELDEST CHILD: Gently the first one puts down its tail
CHILDREN: From Olongo.
ELDEST CHILD: Gently the second one puts down its tail
CHILDREN: From Olongo.
ELDEST CHILD: Gently the third one puts down its tail
YOUNGEST CHILD (*alone*): From Olongo!!!

    There is loud laughter and OGBOINBA *now steps into the circle and picks up the* YOUNGEST CHILD. *The* CHILDREN *surround her, shouting welcome.*

LAKPE: Welcome my sister, welcome Ogboinba.
How the children love you,
They cling to you more than to their own mother.
And how are you? Have you had a busy day?
You look sad, are you tired?
You know what?
Dupe spoke her first word today!
Guess what she said: Mamma, she said,

She said it twice!

I was so excited!

But you look sad, my dear. What is the matter?

I am sure you are tired, after your day's work.

And hungry!

Let me get you some food.

OGBOINBA: No, Lakpe, please, don't bother.

I am all right.

LAKPE: No, no, you will not leave my house without eating.

And we have bushmeat today!

> LAKPE *leaves the room. The* CHILDREN *gather round* OGBOINBA. *They urge her to sing and play with her.* OGBOINBA, *still a bit listless and reluctant, finally gives in.*

OGBOINBA (*sings*): Woru O, woru O, on the farm.

Woru O, woru O, on the river.

Woru who feeds birds with maize.

When I returned home, I complained to my father.

Father beat Woru hard.

Under the banana-tree, under the orange-tree,

How did you get under the pepper shrub?

> LAKPE *enters with the food. The song is interrupted.* LAKPE *motions the* CHILDREN *away. She places a table in front of* OGBOINBA *and places food on water on it.*

LAKPE: Now leave Ogboinba alone, children.

Let her eat.

> LAKPE *sits down a little way away from the table. The* CHILDREN *sit down and keep quiet for a while.* OGBOINBA *starts to eat listlessly. She stops eating; stares in front of her and repeats slowly in a sad voice.*

OGBOINBA: A child is a rare bird.

A child is precious like coral.

You cannot buy a child on the market —

Not with all the money in the world.

One's child is one's child:

The buttocks of one's child cannot be so flat,
That one would fit the beads on another child's waist . . .
She suddenly pushes the food away from her. She jumps up and
bursts out.
I cannot bear it,
I cannot bear it any longer!
To see you swell up with child nearly every two years
To see you surrounded by eight children
And for me to have none. Not even a single one!
I cannot bear to see the happiness in your eyes
To stand by and watch with my shrivelled womb!
I hate myself, my cursed body,
Unable to have even an abortion.
I will not suffer it
I will not bear my shame another day!
I shall return to Woyengi and challenge my fate!

LAKPE: You are mad, Ogboinba,
What will you do!
Have you not chosen your fate yourself?
And don't you know it is irrevocable?
Calm yourself!
Are not my children yours?
Don't they belong to you as much as me?
Ogboinba, I implore you!
Restrain yourself,
Do not utter such terrible words.
See here:
Choose any of my children,
Let it be yours for ever.
Take it away – let me not set eyes on it again:
Only, I beg, you Ogboinba, my friend,
Ogboinba, I implore you,
Do not utter such terrible words again.

OGBOINBA: Do not restrain me!

Lakpe, I warn you!
You do not know the fire in my mind.
I am consumed with envy; it gnaws my heart away
Chews my intestines.
Were I to stay with you and watch your happiness
Much longer, I'd kill your little ones
All – one by one.
I have the power —
To set the fever on their brain
The ulcer on their stomach.
I can make their blood dry up,
Their little limbs wither.
Cursed be the powers I was given!
I fear myself —
I merely have to wish, to kill!
So let me go to Woyengi!
I'll challenge her
And she must recreate my fate!

LAKPE: Ogboinba, I beg you,
   Do not leave us.
We need you! We need your counsel
Your knowledge and protection.
Do not expose my little ones
To all the hazards of the world.
Be satisfied with what you have!
Have you not fame? Power? Respect?
Are you not loved? Envied by many?
What greater life than yours?
Oh look at me!
I have no talents and no gifts.
Help nobody, serve none.
All I can do is to bear children.
Is that so wonderful?
All women can do that!

But you, you are alone
In all your greatness!

OGBOINBA (*now calm but determined*): Lakpe,
I must leave. Nothing can stop me.
Here – keep this charm,
It will protect your children.
For me nothing is left,
But to attempt the impossible.
I may be too little for the other world —
But I am much too big for this one!
My heart is bursting with power:
I must try my strength against Woyengi!
For who else could I measure myself against?
May your children live!
May you live to enjoy them!
May you have grandchildren to bury you!

> OGBOINBA *leaves* LAKPE *and the* CHILDREN *dazed.*
> LAKPE *calls after her, feebly. But* OGBOINBA *has already*
> *reached her house. The lights now fade on* LAKPE'*s house,*
> *and are dimmed on* OGBOINBA *who is speaking incantations:*

OGBOINBA: Werepe – yerepe
Rorowo – worowo
Popondo – godogbodo
Koropo – koporo
Sweetness of rattle pea; bitterness of monkey kola;
Spice of ginger-lily; heat of alligator pepper;
Hardness of palmnut; softness of silk cotton;
Bleeding like flamboyant – limp like 'love is bleeding'.

> *As she is talking two bird-like creatures emerge from the dark-*
> *ness and attach themselves to her. As she leaves the house they*
> *follow close behind.*

CURTAIN

In the forest. OGBOINBA *enters from left, followed by the two spirit powers. She stops for a moment and looks around.* ISEMBI, *king of the forest, enters from the right, dressed like a hunter, but rather more richly adorned. He is followed by two bird-like creatures, who likewise symbolize his spiritual powers.*

ISEMBI: Venture no farther:
   No living being has defied my orders
   No human creature ever penetrated
   My sacred grove.
   Whoever you are – turn back!
OGBOINBA: I listen to no one's command!
   Know, I am Ogboinba,
   Who has no equal in this world.
ISEMBI: Of your powers I have heard.
   Of your strength and deeds.
   But do not overestimate yourself.
   Human charms lose their powers
   In the world of spirits.
   No human being can defy me —
   Let alone a woman!
OGBOINBA: Do not spurn my sex!
   Sexless and dry-wombed
   I stand before you.
   My powers are beyond human reach:
   For they were bought with childlessness!
   I challenge you to a trial of strength!
SEMBI: I wished to spare you —

Now it is too late.
Beware then!
Show what you can do!
But you cannot touch me:
Like hedgehogs, I sting in your hand;
He who approaches me,
Faints, like the dog who foolishly attacks
Olooyunbere, the skink.
And his weapon wriggles impotently
Like a lizard's broken tail.
Beware now:
Feel your movements slow like the potto's,
Your legs thin like the duiker's, snapping under your weight;
Roll in the mud, like tuukú the waterhog;
Feel now the puff-adder's sting in your heart!

> *As* ISEMBI *is speaking his incantations,* OGBOINBA'*s powers detach themselves from her and crawl over to* ISEMBI; *first one, then the other.* OGBOINBA *gets weaker, writhes and falls. But as* ISEMBI *pronounces his last incantation she is beginning her own.*

OGBOINBA (*still on the ground*): Werepe – yerepe
Rorowo – worowo
Popondo – godogbodo
Koropo – koporo.
Lose your sweetness to the rattle pea
And your bitterness to the monkey kola.
Let the ginger-lily drain you of spice,
And the alligator pepper of heat!
Let your bones lose their hardness to the palmnut;
Let your flesh lose its softness to the silk cotton!
Be drained of your sap – like a felled palm-tree!
Bleed like the flamboyant!
Hang limp and helpless like tete oibo,
Like 'love is bleeding' from its stalk!

While she is talking, her powers return one by one and then ISEMBI'*s powers leave him, and he totters and falls.* OGBOINBA *has regained her strength with her powers. Now she leaps on to the helpless* ISEMBI.

OGBOINBA: Fool!
I will spare your life, though you don't deserve it!
Stay in your forest: a king without power;
An impotent ruler, writhing like the broken tail
Of a lizard!

OGBOINBA *moves out triumphantly – followed by all the powers.*

CURTAIN

The scene has changed very quickly to a wild sea coast. OGBOINBA
enters from the left, followed by the four powers. OLOKUN
*enters from the right to challenge her. He is followed by his own
powers.* OLOKUN, *king of the sea, is dressed in a magnificent
gown studded with cowrie shells.*

OLOKUN: No farther, woman —
  The end of your journey has come!
  I am Olokun, king of all the waters on earth!
  I am king of the river and king of the source;
  I am king of the lagoon and king of the ocean.
  No living creature must cross this water:
  Such is Woyengi's command
  And I am here to carry out her wish!
OGBOINBA: Do you know who I am?
  If Isembi could not make me turn back,
  Why then should you?
  Have you not heard of Ogboinba?
OLOKUN: Your powers are known to me
  And so is your pride.
  Still – let me advise you:
  Do not defy Woyengi's command!
  No human being shall cross this water
  No being – human or spirit —
  Has ever defied my command!
OGBOINBA: What if I am the first?
  Complacent king of the waters!
  You'll find your match today:

I challenge you to a trial of strength!
Now let us see, if your magic can touch
The wombless woman,
Ogboinba, who has no equal.

OLOKUN: Proud creature!
Would you defy Woyengi herself?
Yet you cannot withstand even me:
See the waters closing in on you!
Already the jelly-fish burns on your chest —
A monstrous nightmare.
Already the shark is on his back
In hot pursuit!
Fear you his grinning jaw?
You bury your frightened head in the sand
Like the mudfish; wriggle, trembling,
Between the rocks like an eel!
Already you jerk on the hook like the stupid carp;
You flap your fins like the helpless flounder
Thrown on the beach; while your blood trickles
Cold and white from your pierced snout into the sand!

> OGBOINBA *has lost all her powers during the incantation.
> Now she is wriggling on the ground, as if in pain. But as*
> OLOKUN — *followed by the six powers — proudly tries to
> approach her, she begins her own incantations, at first still
> lying on the ground.*

OGBOINBA: Werepe – yerepe
Rorowo – worowo
Popondo – godogbodo
Koropo – koporo.
Lose your sweetness to the rattle pea
And your bitterness to the monkey kola.
Let the ginger-lily drain you of spice,
And the alligator pepper of heat!
Let your bones lose their hardness to the palmnut

Let your flesh lose its softness to the silk cotton!
Be drained of your sap – like a felled palm-tree!
Bleed like the flamboyant!
Hang limp and helpless like tete oibo,
Like 'love is bleeding' from its stalk!

> *During the incantation some of the powers return to her.*
> OGBOINBA *now stands erect, facing* OLOKUN, *who has*
> *retreated again. The powers are equally divided.* OGBOINBA
> *pauses as if to see whether* OLOKUN *has further incantations*
> *at hand. But* OLOKUN *is silent. Suddenly* OGBOINBA
> *breaks out into a new incantation.*

OGBOINBA: You cannot touch me:
Like hedgehogs, I sting in your hand!
He who approaches me,
Faints, like the dog who foolishly attacks
Olooyunbere, the skink!
And his weapon wriggles impotently,
Like a lizard's broken tail!
Beware now:
Feel your movements slow like the potto's
Your legs thin like the duiker's, snapping under your weight;
Roll in the mud, like tuukú the waterhog;
Feel now the puff-adder's sting in your heart!

> OGBOINBA *has gained all the powers now.* OLOKUN *has*
> *fallen helplessly to the ground.* OGBOINBA *stands over him*
> *triumphantly.*

OGBOINBA: Flap your fins then, like the helpless flounder
Thrown on the beach!
No one can stand between me and Woyengi!
Helpless king of the waters —
Frightened now, of your own sharks!

                    CURTAIN

The Kingdom of the Cock.
The scene has changed very quickly into a strange, bleak landscape,
full of strange shapes. OGBOINBA *enters from the left, followed*
by the full host of her powers. The COCK *storms in noisily;*
he is huge and his costume is flaming red.

COCK: Ogboinba —
    Master your pride!
    You have vanquished Isembi,
    Olokun you have subdued.
    But you can go no farther!
    This is the last kingdom of those who die
    Death alone can lead you farther!
    Here all the living must return.
OGBOINBA: As Isembi and Olokun
    Are now impotent and helpless kings,
    The ridicule of their kingdoms,
    So will I reduce you too to size.
    I will pluck your proud feathers
    One by one! And you will run to hide
    Your pimply body exposed!
    Don't try to stop me then!
    For to Woyengi I must,
    To meet her in the greatest trial of all!
    Only once do I want to vanquish her:
    One single time only force her will,
    Bend her powers to my own designs.
    For she must recreate my fate.

But once my body swells up
And I feel the child kicking under my heart —
I will renounce my powers:
Incantations, potion, poisons, medicines —
Will be of use to me no further.
Let her but give life to my withered body
And I will submit body and soul
To her every command.

COCK: Madwoman!
Will you change the order of the world?
Will you break the laws
That hold the earth together?
And even if you succeeded
Even if you could vanquish Woyengi,
Know you not that it would be the end of the world
And the child you would bear
Would be the last of children
Ever to be born?

OGBOINBA: Let it be the last or the first —
Who cares?
And if the sun crushes into the ocean
And the sea begins to boil,
If the stars fall like burning hail
And set the earth alight,
Who cares?
I must have my child,
I must have my fight with Woyengi.
My heart is bursting with power,
My brain is charged with incantations —
Get out of the way, proud Cock,
Before I pluck you!

Werepe – yerepe
Rorowo – worowo

Popondo – godogbodo
Koropo – koporo.
Lose your sweetness to the rattle pea.
And your bitterness to the monkey kola.
Let the ginger-lily drain you of spice,
And the alligator pepper of heat.
Be drained of your sap – like a felled palm-tree!
Bleed like the flamboyant!
Hang limp and helpless like tete oibo,
Like 'love is bleeding' from its stalk.

COCK (*unmoved and unaffected*): You waste your breath!
In the last kingdom of those who die,
Your words are wind.
Do you command no stronger words?

OGBOINBA (*rattled, but determined*): Beware:
You cannot touch me:
Like hedgehogs, I sting in your hand;
He who approaches me faints,
Like the dog, who foolishly attacks
Olooyunbere, the skink.
Beware now:
Feel your movements slow like the potto's,
Your legs thin like the duiker's, snapping under your weight;
Feel now the cobra's poison in your veins,
The puff-adder's sting in your heart!

> *This time the* COCK *has been hit. His powers have gone over to* OGBOINBA. *He flutters breathlessly on the ground. But he recovers and speaks his own incantations.*

COCK: Let the weaverbird strip you of your bright coat,
Let the kingfisher possess your wealth.
Let the bulbul steal your song
And the red-tailed parrot your speech!
Let the hornbill crack your wisdom in his beak;
Let the rust-coloured coockal peck up your magic.

And what remains of your life,
Now quivering and naked —
The fluttering sunbird will drink it
Like nectar from a flower.

The COCK *has recovered and has sent* OGBOINBA *staggering back. But she now rises once more to pronounce her last incantation.*

OGBOINBA: Beware proud bird —
The waters now are closing in on you.
Already the jelly-fish burns on your chest —
A monstrous nightmare.
Already the shark is on his back,
In hot pursuit!
Fear you his grinning jaw?
Already you jerk on the hook like the stupid carp:
You flap your fins like the helpless flounder
Thrown on the beach; while your blood trickles
Cold and white from your pierced snout into the sand.

The COCK *is vanquished.* OGBOINBA *stands over him, triumphant, plucking his feathers and scattering them about.*

OGBOINBA: Cockerel,
What happened to the fire on your head?
The trumpet in your throat?
The spurs on your feet?
Your wives will have a nice surprise
To see you now bereaved of feathers,
All goosepimply and blue.

CURTAIN

SCENE VI

Heaven.

WOYENGI *sits on the throne, as in scene one.* SWORDBEARERS
and CREATURES *stand by her side as before.*

WOYENGI: My creatures approach:
 The world is waiting for you!
 Come now and choose your lives,
 But choose wisely.
 Nobody can eat the words
 He will speak here and now.
 Approach then my creatures
 And choose your fate:
 Whether man or woman you wish to be,
 What manner of life you wish to lead,
 What to achieve on earth, how long to live —
 And finally – most difficult choice of all —
 You must select your death.
   The first CREATURE *steps forwards and kneels. But before
   he can speak* OGBOINBA *rushes on to the stage, followed by
   her eight powers.*
OGBOINBA: Stop! Hold your words!
 Woyengi, I have conquered the world!
 The impossible have I achieved:
 'The last kingdom of those who die'
 I left behind – the first of all mortal beings
 To cross the great threshold alive.
 Woyengi, now beware!
 The powers you allowed me

Were too great for yonder world!
They nearly burst my heart —
They split my head!
So here I am to challenge you in heaven:
Do the impossible now,
As I have done the impossible:
Eat your words, and recreate my fate!
If you refuse,
Come let us match our powers!
I feel elated now, triumphant, and
Victorious!
All the magic of Isembi and Olokun
Yes, even the powerful charms of the Cock,
Are at my side.
Woyengi: remake my womb!
Let the seed not rot in my belly,
Let not envy eat up my heart
Let me not destroy Lakpe's children!
I will command you just this once, Woyengi,
Before all powers I renounce!
Woyengi!
Reshape my fate, my life, my womb!

WOYENGI (*trembling with rage*): Mad creature!
How dare you challenge me?
I, who made the world with my hands?
Who placed the sun in the sky
Who lets the Niger flow into the sea
And across the sky?
I, who allowed you to grow in the womb,
Who opened your mouth and allowed you to speak?
Have you forgotten
That I am the source of all powers?

    Even during these words OGBOINBA *has been stripped of all powers. She now stands trembling and whimpering*

before WOYENGI, *her hands raised in an attitude of prayer.*
You asked for more
Than any other living soul!
I granted all.
Miserable, helpless creature,
Did you really think,
The powers I lent you
Enabled you to invade heaven?
You are not fit to live!

WOYENGI *grabs one of the ceremonial swords from a* SWORDBEARER *and hurls it at* OGBOINBA. *She misses and* OGBOINBA *flees in wild terror.*

CURTAIN

Scene VII

A quick succession of scenes ending with LAKPE's *house.*

OGBOINBA *is seen running fearfully through the Kingdom of the Cock. Blackout, and then she appears running through the sea-shore; blackout again, and she is seen rushing through the forest. One more blackout, and the scene is now* LAKPE's *house (Scene II).*

OGBOINBA *bursts in from left, runs to* LAKPE, *and hides under her wide lappa.* LAKPE *is obviously pregnant.* WOYENGI *appears from left, pursuing* OGBOINBA. *She looks around for a few seconds, then goes up to* LAKPE *and stares into her eyes.*

WOYENGI: So there you are hiding!
    In a pregnant woman's eyes!
    Clever you are to the last,
    Knowing I will not break my own law
    And hurt a pregnant woman!
    Well then, so be it!
    Live you in the woman's eyes.
    But know that never more
    Will you lead a life of your own,
    Never be given another beginning.
    May you lead an existence of fear
    Peeping out of other people's eyes.
    And may you be a warning to mankind:
    When they look at each other's eyes,
    They will see you staring at them
    And remember your mad adventure.
    Never more shall man be so bold!

*WOYENGI turns to go off centre and the lights fade out on her.
As LAKPE and the children look after her, the rest of the cast
gradually crowd on the stage. As WOYENGI disappears in the
background, the huge sun from Scene I slowly descends and the
crowd fall on their knees.*

CHORUS: Woyengi,
  Mother of the world,
  The world lies in your hand,
  As it was on the day you made it
  In your loneliness.
  You command the sun and the moon.
  You made thousands of creatures
  From your single form.
  You create the child in the womb,
  Made the seed flow in man
  And the blood flow in woman.
  Woyengi, mother of the world,
  Your feet walk the earth,
  While your head towers in the sky.

CURTAIN

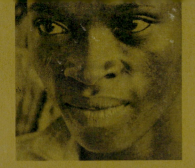

OBOTUNDE IJIMERE was born in Otan Aiyegbaju, Western Nigeria, in 1930. After leaving secondary school he joined Duro Ladipo's theatre company, but soon discovered he had no talent for acting. He attended Ulli Beier's extra-mural writers' workshop in Oshogbo, and followed his advice to write in English rather than in Yoruba. Apart from the plays in this volume he has written some short stories (he is not very satisfied with the result) and several other plays, including one in pidgin, *The Fall of Man*, specially written for Theatre Express, the Lagos-based theatre group.

Theatre in the Yoruba language is mostly a kind of opera in which the songs are rehearsed while the dialogue is improvised. The first to break away from this tradition was Duro Ladipo, and his plays have had considerable influence on Obotunde Ijimere. This volume contains *The Imprisonment of Obatala*, *Everyman* and *Woyengi*, which is based on an Ijaw tale. *Obatala* is based on a Yoruba myth, which explores the philosophy of Yoruba *orisha* worship. *Everyman* is an adaptation of Hugo von Hofmanthal's play, but the basic theme has been rethought entirely in Yoruba terms: thus the Christian mythology of Heaven and Hell has been replaced by the Yoruba concept of reincarnation. Everyman's greatest punishment would be to be 'thrown on the heaven of potshers' – that is, never to return to this earth again.

The cover photograph is from a batik by Suzanne Wenger

 African Writers Series
An H·E·B Paperback

Date Due

Demco 38-297